GARDENER'S QUESTION TIME

DAVID SQUIRE

CONTENTS

Introduction 2

Flowers 4

Vegetables 36

Fruit 50

Trees and Hedges 56

Lawns 60

Index 64

This edition published 1988 by
Octopus Books Limited
Michelin House
81 Fulham Road
London SW3 6RB

INTRODUCTION

With a weekly mail bag that numbers well into three figures, I know how confusing this gardening lark can be. Readers and viewers and listeners are often left baffled in spite of attempts to make things clear, so they put pen to paper and ask for their problem to be solved personally. This little book should most certainly save on the stamps and the stationery. Here are the answers to hundreds of niggling questions, set out in a form that's easy to understand and, equally important, in a way that makes the questions in question easy to find. In some cases it's a term or description that's puzzling. What's an herbaceous perennial? What is meant by N P K? Or it may be a tricky part of the garden – one which is in shade or which has acid soil – that needs planting up with suitable shrubs. The answers are here – simply and briefly set down so that they are easy to follow. Certain questions make up what you might call a list of 'Chart Toppers'; for example, there's one about plants to grow on a north-facing garage which needs brightening up. David Squire also offers solutions to questions such as: How can heavy clay soil be made easier to dig? How can I have colour in my garden all the year round? When and how should weedkillers be applied to lawns? It's easy to be dogmatic in gardening, and to offer one answer to a problem as though it were the only possible solution. Life isn't like that, and, unfortunately, neither is gardening. Just as there's more than one way of skinning a cat, there's usually more than one way of covering up a dreary garden shed, or planting up a garden pool, or providing a bit of winter colour. Where necessary, the author has given you plenty of choice so that your garden need not be a carbon copy of your neighbour's. That said, some operations have been carried out in a certain way for donkey's years, and so they are given here in traditional form. This isn't simply stick-in-the-mudiness, it's just that the method described is one that, over the years, gardeners have discovered gives the best results in most gardens. Once you've mastered the basic technique there's absolutely no reason why you shouldn't play around with it a bit. In your unique circumstances you may be able to succeed where others have failed. So whatever your problem, dip into the following pages to look for a solution. There may be some questions that remain unanswered, for this is no definitive work, but I'll be very surprised if, as you're looking up one problem, the answer to another isn't magically solved as your eye flits across the lines.

FLOWERS

PERENNIALS

What is an herbaceous perennial?

This is a plant that each year develops stems, leaves and flowers, and dies down to a crown of dormant buds at soil-level in autumn. The plant is perpetuated from season to season by its roots which are hardy enough to survive the winter in a dormant state.

Below *A traditional herbaceous border. Although at their best in midsummer, such borders can be planned to provide pockets of colour in the garden all through the year.*

What is a mixed border?

This is when many different types of plants are grown in the same border to achieve a variety of effects and a maximum display of colour throughout the year. The plants can include narrow and upright conifers to bring height and coloured foliage the year through, flowering trees and shrubs to give seasonal interest, variegated trees and shrubs for year-round interest, or spring and summer attraction from deciduous types. Herbaceous plants play an important role and help to create interest before the more permanent residents such as trees and shrubs are fully established. And more short-lived plants such as annuals, which grow, flower and die in one year, and biennials, which flower and die in their second year, fill in bare areas that inevitably occur in all borders. Bulbs bring extra bright spots of colour.

I have only a small border for herbaceous plants. Is it better to plant just one specimen of each type I wish to grow, or to plant several of each type and therefore not have such a wide selection?

Herbaceous plants are best seen in bold groupings rather than dotted singly here and there. Set them in clusters of three of a kind, as odd numbered arrangements are easier to arrange and look more attractive in a border than twos or fours which can look awkward.

When preparing and planting the border, first sketch it on graph paper. Transfer the shapes on the plan to the prepared border, using a trickle of sharp sand to indicate the outlines. The positions of the plants within these shapes can be indicated with small sticks. This ensures that the finished border will be evenly planted, and not appear sparse or congested at one end.

Q

I have a narrow border against a wall and wish to have an early-flowering herbaceous plant interplanted with tulips and daffodils so that it becomes a 'little-effort' flower bed. What do you suggest?

A

Choose plants with slender stems 'lightly clad' with smallish leaves that will not smother the daffodils and tulips. One of the most suitable is *Doronicum plantagineum*. There are several varieties to choose from, including 'Miss Mason' at 450 mm (1½ ft) high and with bright yellow flowers, 'Harpur Crewe' with golden-yellow flowers, and 'Spring Beauty' at 380 mm (15 inches) high with double, deep yellow flowers. Others include *Dicentra* 'Pearl Drops', 300 mm (1 ft), and *Dicentra spectabilis* 'Alba', 450 mm (1½ ft), both of which have arching sprays of white locket-like flowers; *Helleborus foetidus*, 450 mm (1½ ft), valued for its handsome, figured leaves and intriguing, nodding, greenish flowers; *Helleborus orientalis*, 300 mm (1 ft), whose saucer-shaped blooms range from greenish-white to plum and pink; and *Euphorbia griffithii* 'Fireglow', 600 mm (2 ft), a spreading beauty with fiery red heads that contrast effectively with daffodils. All bloom in early spring.

Q

I am planning an herbaceous border and would like to know which plants need staking and which do not. Advice, please.

A

Those which do need staking to avoid wind bending and breaking shoots include *Achillea* 'Gold Plate', delphiniums, the taller herbaceous geraniums such as *Geranium psilostemon* and Oriental Poppies.

The art of staking is to make the supports invisible. Pushing twiggy sticks into the soil while the plants are quite small so that the foliage grows and hides them is the best method. A few plants, such as delphiniums with tall stems, are best supported with strong bamboo canes and green string. Enclose clumps with three or four stout canes inserted securely, sloping slightly outwards, and linked with two tiers of soft string. Alternatively use stakes which are hooked together to enclose shoots. By

INCREASING HERBACEOUS PLANTS

Q

What is the easiest way to increase herbaceous plants?

A

During autumn or spring – the latter in cold areas – dig around large and established clumps and lift them on to the surface. Insert two garden forks back to back in the clump and lever it apart. Replant only young pieces from around the outside of the clump, and discard the old central part.

Border perennials with long tap roots (single tapering carrot-like roots), such as Bleeding Heart (*Dicentra spectabilis*), anchusa, Oriental Poppy and gypsophila, may also be increased from root cuttings. These are 75–100 mm (3–4 inch) vertical root sections, sliced off level at the top and sloping at the bottom, so you know which is which and don't make the mistake of planting them upside down. They are taken in autumn and planted vertically in deep pots of gritty potting compost with their tops just beneath the surface. Overwintered in a cold frame, new growth appears the following spring.

Border Phlox (*Phlox paniculata*) is also increased from root cuttings when stem eelworm has infested the plant and curled its leaves. The pest remains in the stem, never travelling to the roots, so these stay healthy. In this instance 50–75 mm (2–3 inch) long sections of the thread-like roots are laid flat in a pot of soil and covered to a depth of 12 mm (½ inch). If these are taken in the autumn and overwintered in a cold frame, new plants appear the next spring.

Above *Dividing an herbaceous plant. Push two forks, back to back, into the crown of the plant and force the forks apart. The size of the forks used depends on the size of the clump to be divided.*

the way, fewer and fewer herbaceous plants need supporting as plant breeders develop stronger and lower growing forms that need less attention.

Self-supporting candidates for an herbaceous border have an altogether more robust constitution, with flower stems that flex but do not break in gusty weather. Good examples are purple and white flowered Bear's Breech (*Acanthus spinosus*), rose, pink and white varieties of *Anemone hupehensis*, silver-leaved *Artemisia lactiflora*, mauve-blue *Aster frikartii*, Red Hot Poker (kniphofia), Border Phlox in many colours including red, orange, pink and white, pinkish-red sidalcea, orange-red crocosmias and architectural-leaved rodgersias and phormiums.

HARDY & HALF-HARDY ANNUALS

Q

What is the difference between a half-hardy annual and a hardy annual?

A

Both grow, flower and die within the year, but a half-hardy annual is frost-tender so it is raised in heat in late winter and early spring and planted out in late May or early June when nights are no longer frosty. Examples are zinnias, petunias, heliotrope and lobelia.

Hardy annuals have a tougher nature and are sown outdoors in late March or April to flower freely throughout the summer. Included among them are Marigolds (*calendula*), Candytuft, Clarkia and Californian Poppy (*eschscholzia*).

Most half-hardy annuals may be sown directly where they will flower, in late May. They will bloom much later than early spring-raised plants but yield a welcome bonus of colour in late summer. In warmer, south-western parts of the country many half-hardy annuals can be sown where they will flower, in April or May.

Below Lobelia erinus, *grown as a half-hardy annual, is often used in bedding schemes.*

Q

What are biennials and how are they grown?

A

These are plants that are sown one year to flower the following one, then die. The seeds are sown in a seedbed during early summer, germinated and grown into young plants, then transferred to their flowering positions in autumn. In extremely cold areas, cover them with cloches in winter. Remove the cloches in spring and set the plants in their flowering positions.

Q

How can I prevent my annual seeds being raked up by birds as soon as they are sown?

A

There are two easy methods of protecting your seeds. After they have been sown place brushwood over them, removing the sticks as soon as the seeds show signs of life. Alternatively, you could use a chemical bird deterrent.

Stretching black cotton over the whole bed is sometimes recommended, but it can cripple birds if it becomes entangled with their feet.

Incidentally, if sowing annuals on sloping ground, prevent erosion in wet weather by covering the sown area with fine plastic-covered mesh netting. Remove the netting as soon as seedlings push through the soil.

Q

I have several flower beds under my windows. Please suggest a range of seed-raised plants for both spring and summer fragrance.

A

Annuals and biennials are ideal for this purpose, and there is a wide range to choose from.
Wallflower (*Cheiranthus cheiri*)
　Height: 200–600 mm (8–24 inches)
　　　　　(range of heights)
　Spread: 250–380 mm (10–15 inches)
　　　　　(range of spreads)

A hardy perennial grown as a hardy biennial, and one of the most popular late spring-flowering plants. The colour range is extensive, including white, pink, red, yellow and orange.

Sweet William (*Dianthus barbatus*)
   Height: 300–450 mm (1–1½ ft)
   Spread: 300–380 mm (12–15 inches)

A perennial usually grown as a hardy biennial. The range of colours is extensive, and flowers appear during June and July.

Candytuft (*Iberis umbellata*)
   Height: 150–300 mm (6–12 inches)
   Spread: 250–300 mm (10–12 inches)

A hardy annual with clusters of purple, rose-red and white flowers 50 mm (2 inches) wide from June to September.

Virginian Stock (*Malcolmia maritima*)
   Height: 200–250 mm (8–10 inches)
   Spread: 150–200 mm (6–8 inches)

A hardy annual – ideal for sowing in combination with the Night-scented Stock – with flowers in a range of colours from May to August. They flower about four weeks after being sown.

Night-scented Stock (*Matthiola bicornis*)
   Height: 300–380 mm (12–15 inches)
   Spread: 200–250 mm (8–10 inches)

A hardy annual, known for its spikes of lilac-coloured fragrant flowers during July and August. As its common name suggests, it smells sweetest in the evenings.

Above *Sweet William* (Dianthus barbatus) *is a popular choice for flower beds, combining bright colours with exquisite fragrance.*

ANNUALS FOR SHADE

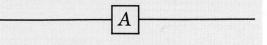
Q

My neighbour's new fence shades my annual border for part of the day. Which annuals are suited for such a position?

A

Try any of the following biennials:

Canterbury Bell (*Campanula medium*) (*pictured left*) 'Bells of Holland' in blue, mauve, rose and white, 380 mm (15 inches).

Foxglove (*Digitalis purpurea*) 'Suttons Excelsior Hybrids', colours range from cream through pink to purple, 1·5 m (5 ft).

Forget-me-not (*Myosotis sylvatica*) 'Royal Blue', intense rich blue flowers, 300 mm (1 ft); 'Carmine King', pure carmine flowers, 200 mm (8 inches).

Pansy (*Viola* × *wittrockiana*) F1 hybrids include 'Imperial Orange Prince', orange with a dark blotch; 'Azure Blue', clear blue with yellow eye; and 'Universal Mixture' representing twelve distinct colours. The F1 hybrids grow to 150–230 mm (6–9 inches).

BULBS, CORMS & TUBERS

Q

I would like to grow daffodils in an area of short grass. Can you recommend some eye-catching varieties?

A

There are many to choose from, but some of the finest are the trumpet varieties: golden-yellow 'Dutch Master', 'Golden Harvest', yellow and white 'Queen of Bicolours' and ice-white 'Mount Hood'. All grow to around 450 mm (1½ ft) tall.

Among the short-cupped forms are orange and white 'Margaret Mitchell' and 'La Riante', the latter growing to 350 mm (14 inches), the former to 425 mm (17 inches) tall.

Especially appealing are the split corona (orchid flowering) varieties in which the trumpet (corona) has been bred to lie flat on the perianth (outer ring of petals) and cover it for more than two thirds.

Dwarf forms have some exciting contenders and the Hoop Petticoat Daffodil (*Narcissus bulbocodium*) is a 100–150 mm (4–6 inch) delight. Its 25 mm (1 inch) wide yellow 'crinolines' appear in February and March. Another neat performer is *N. cyclamineus*. Growing to 200 mm (8 inches), this small golden daffodil is distinguished by its tubular trumpet being offset by attractively reflexed petals. It also flowers in very early spring. But it is important to remember that these small daffodils only naturalize well in short, fine grass.

Q

Apart from naturalizing bulbs in grass, how else can you feature them to enhance the garden?

A

For formal arrangements, you could interplant hyacinths with their stiff, soldier-like stance to contrast effectively with the globular heads of tulips.

Blue-flowered muscari look magnificent lighting up the ground beneath a beech hedge still in its russet-brown leaved winter garb.

Golden-flowered daffodils look resplendent against a red brick wall.

Double early tulips in pink, red or white create an eye-catching feature planted in troughs or windowboxes; white, blue and yellow crocuses peeping from the cups of a strawberry barrel make an attractive terrace or patio feature. Botanical tulips – *Tulipa chrysantha* in red and yellow; *T. eichleri* in scarlet, and golden *T. batalinii* are ideal for illuminating pockets in a rock garden.

Winter Aconites (*Eranthis hyemalis*) display their shining, golden cup-like flowers at the same time as *Iris histrioides* 'Major' sports its rich blue flowers and each complements the other.

Another winning combination is achieved by interplanting pale blue *Crocus tomasinianus* with nodding, white-flowered snowdrops, both of which flower during February and March.

BULBS FOR BENEATH TREES

For dry, shaded areas:
Cyclamen hederifolium (syn. *C. neapolitanum*)
Height: 100 mm (4 in)
Beautifully marbled green and silver leaves, and mauve to pale pink flowers August to November.
Endymion hispanicus
Height: 300 mm (1 ft)
Bluebell-like flowers during late spring, with forms in blue, pink and white.
Endymion nonscriptus
Height: 300 mm (1 ft)
This is the English Bluebell or Wild Hyacinth, with late spring blue flowers. Pink and white forms are also available.

PLANTING HYACINTHS

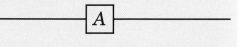

Q

When planting hyacinths in bowls, should I cover the tops of the bulbs with bulb fibre or leave them uncovered?

A

It is essential to leave the tips exposed. Place bulb fibre in the base of the pot and work evenly around the bulbs. Do not pack the fibre too firmly or the roots will force up the bulbs. Bring the fibre to 12 mm (½ inch) below the rim of the container, leaving the tips uncovered.

Remember, when interposing one colour with another, it should either blend or contrast. Clashes are best avoided, as are greatly varying heights; beware of foliage which differs widely so one plant dominates with its wide spreading leaves, while the other's slender delicate leaves are swamped and beware also of flowering times which fail to coincide.

What should I do when the foliage on my bulbs dies down?

The leaves are best left alone to die down naturally, returning the food value in them to the bulbs. Often the long leaves of daffodils can be a problem. These are often doubled back and held in position with an elastic-band but this is not good practice as it restricts the flow of sap to the bulb.

It is better to be patient until six weeks have elapsed after flowering. The leaves can then be cut off without impairing next year's crop of flowers.

I would like to plant my large wooden tub with a blue-flowered plant that blossoms in summer. It's for a sun-drenched patio. What do you suggest?

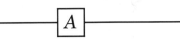

For a strong impact choose *Agapanthus* 'Headbourne Hybrids'. They form a large clump and require a warm position. These plants look especially effective when set against a white wall. Although of the lily family, the agapanthus is often included in herbaceous catalogues. It grows some 750 mm (2½ ft) tall and its handsome rush-like foliage complements impressive stems topped with large almost globular heads of deep blue, trumpet-shaped flowers in July and August.

Hydrangeas form a dominant display and are especially useful for creating late summer colour. Choose *Hydrangea macrophylla* and use one of the large-flowered mop-headed hortensia types. To ensure blue varieties remain blue, the compost must be either neutral or slightly acid. In alkaline (chalky) composts almost all the blue varieties turn pink or reddish-purple.

Above *The graceful erythronium, which flourishes in slightly shaded positions.*

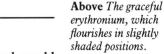

I have a patch of semi-woodland and would like to grow some shade-lovers to carpet the ground. What do you recommend?

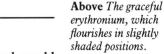

Choice bulbs that enjoy cool, moist soil and dappled shade include the violet, pink and white Dog's Tooth Violet (*Erythronium dens-canis*), its cousin the white American Trout Lily (*E. revolutum*) and the yellow *E. tuolumnense*. These flower in March.

Wind Flowers (anemones), blooming in early spring, love deep, leafy soil and *Anemone blanda* 'Atrocoerulea' in rich blue and the extraordinary cerise and white-zoned *A. blanda* 'Radar' should colonize well.

Primroses and hellebores revel in light shade, and finest among the latter are *Helleborus orientalis* in rich wine colours and white, and *H. atrorubens*, valued for its deep plum-coloured blooms. *Helleborus orientalis* flowers during February and March, while *H. atrorubens* creates colour from January to March or April.

SHRUBS

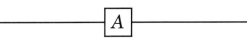

How and when do I prune my Butterfly Bush?

This hardy deciduous shrub (*Buddleia davidii*), which attracts butterflies, is a vigorous plant which produces its handsome, tapering blooms mainly during July and August. These are borne on wood produced the same year, so you should prune the shrub in spring before new leaves develop, cutting back all growths produced during the previous year to within 50 mm (2 inches) of the old wood. This keeps the bush low, with plenty of flowers.

Right Chimonanthus praecox, *a shrub with strongly fragrant flowers.*

Please suggest a late-flowering, hardy shrub.

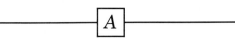

A good choice would be the deciduous July to October flowering *Hibiscus syriacus*. It displays beautiful 75 mm (3 inch) wide flowers with pronounced central bosses. It grows 1·6–2·4 m (6–8 ft) high and 1·2–1·8 m (4–6 ft) wide. A wide range of varieties is available, including 'Blue Bird' (mid-blue, with large red centres), 'Woodbridge' (rose-pink), and 'Snowdrift' (white).

Below Hibiscus syriacus *bears large hollyhock-like flowers from July to October.*

I want to form a winter-flowering shrub garden with scented flowers. What do you suggest?

You can choose from the following selection:
Lonicera × purpusii
   Height: 1·5–1·8 m (5–6 ft)
   Spread: 1·5–1·8 m (5–6 ft)
This deciduous shrub, known as the winter-flowering honeysuckle, bears lemon-scented, 12–18 mm (½–¾ inch) long, creamy-white flowers from December to March.
Viburnum farreri (**syn. *V. fragrans***)
   Height: 2·7–3·5 m (9–12 ft)
   Spread: 2·4–3 m (8–10 ft)
A deciduous shrub with richly-scented, pink-tinged, white flowers in pendant clusters on bare stems from November to March.
Viburnum × burkwoodii
   Height: 1·8–2·4 m (6–8 ft)
   Spread: 2·1–3 m (7–10 ft)
A beautiful evergreen shrub with sweetly-scented, waxy, white flowers that are pink when in bud.
Chimonanthus praecox (**syn. *C. fragrans***)
   Height: 1·8–2·4 m (6–8 ft)
   Spread: 1·5–2·1 m (5–7 ft)
This is the well-known winter sweet, a deciduous shrub with cup-shaped flowers, bearing yellow outer petals and short, purple inner ones from December to February. It looks particularly effective when trained against a wall, perhaps creating colour outside your lounge.

GOLDEN BORDER SHRUBS

I am planning a golden border. Can you recommend a few golden-leaved shrubs that I can use to bring height and focal points to the border?

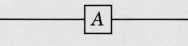

There are many you can choose from; some are evergreen and variegated, others are deciduous. The following ones are very reliable as well as attractive:

Elaeagnus pungens **'Maculata'**
  Height: 1·8–3 m (6–10 ft)
  Spread: 2·4–3 m (8–10 ft)
A distinctive, slow-growing, evergreen shrub with leathery leaves appearing to have been splashed with gold.

Philadelphus coronarius **'Aureus'**
  Height: 1·8–2·4 m (6–8 ft)
  Spread: 1·5–2·1 m (5–7 ft)
A deciduous shrub with a bush nature and bright golden-yellow leaves. Incidentally, it is particularly useful as it does well in dry soils and semi-shade.

Sambucus racemosa **'Plumosa Aurea'**
  Height: 2·1–3 m (7–10 ft)
  Spread: 1·8–2·4 m (6–8 ft)
A beautiful, slow-growing, deciduous shrub with finely-cut golden leaves. The whole plant has a somewhat wispy and feathery appearance that adds to its attractiveness. It looks especially effective at the back of a border, creating a colour contrast for dark-coloured plants.

Above Elaeagnus pungens *'Maculata'. Being evergreen, this shrub enlivens the garden all year round with its gold-splashed foliage.*

I want to brighten my garden in autumn and winter with a few berried shrubs. Have you any suggestions?

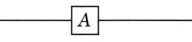

Fortunately, there are many to choose from. In some cases, you will need to have both male and female plants present before berries are produced. In other cases, both sexes exist on one plant, enabling it to produce berries on its own. Plants to try include:

Aucuba japonica **'Picturata'**
  Height: 1·8–3 m (6–10 ft)
  Spread: 1·5–2·4 m (5–8 ft)
A rounded, evergreen shrub with leathery, shiny golden leaves rimmed with green. Round, bright scarlet berries are borne on female plants from autumn to spring.

Checkerberry, Partridge-berry, Winter-green (*Gaultheria procumbens*)
  Height: 100–150 mm (4–6 inches)
  Spread: 900 mm–1·5 m (3–5 ft)
A soil-hugging, evergreen shrub with shiny, dark green leaves and bright red, round berries in autumn and throughout winter.

Sea Buckthorn (*Hippophae rhamnoides*)
  Height: 1·8–2·7 m (6–9 ft)
  Spread: 1·8–2·4 m (6–8 ft)
A hardy, deciduous, bushy shrub, mainly grown for its round, bright orange berries during autumn and winter. They are clustered thickly around the shoots.

Skimmia × **'Foremanii'**
  Height: 900 mm–1·2 m (3–4 ft)
  Spread: 900 mm–1·2 m (3–4 ft)
A beautiful, slow-growing, hardy evergreen shrub which displays fragrant star-like, creamy-white flowers and bright red berries throughout the winter months.

Snowberry (*Symphoricarpos albus*)
  Height: 1·5–1·8 m (5–6 ft)
  Spread: 1·5–2·1 m (5–7 ft)
A well-known, hardy, deciduous shrub with pink urn-shaped flowers during summer, followed by white, round berries throughout late autumn and into winter. This shrub is superb for scrambling and peeping over a low brick wall, and looks extremely striking in a front garden.

ROSES

Above Rosa xanthina *'Canary Bird', with its clear yellow flowers, makes an attractive hedge.*

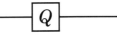

Please suggest a vigorous rose that will form a large hedge.

There are many types to choose from. Many are species types such as *Rosa rugosa*. 'Alba' grows to a height of 1.5–2.1 m (5–7 ft) with a spread of 1.2–1.5 m (4–5 ft). It has wrinkled foliage and 75 mm (3 inch) wide heavily scented, white flowers in June, blooming intermittently to autumn. Set the plants 600–750 mm (2–2½ ft) apart. The clustered-flowered (floribunda) 'Queen Elizabeth' with clear, double, pink, scented flowers is also ideal. Set the plants 900 mm (3 ft) apart.

MORE ROSES FOR HEDGES

Rosa xanthina 'Canary Bird'
  Height: 1·5–1·8 m (5–6 ft)
  Spread: 1·5 m (5 ft)
The semi-double, bright-yellow flowers are borne profusely during May and June. Space plants 600 mm (2 ft) apart.

Sweetbriar or Eglantine (*Rosa rubiginosa*)
  Height: 1·8–2·4 m (6–8 ft)
  Spread: 1·5–1·8 m (5–6 ft)
Bright-pink 40 mm (1½ inch) flowers and sweet-smelling leaves. Space 750 mm (2½ ft) apart.

Rosa rubrifolia
  Height: 1·8–2·1 m (6–7 ft)
  Spread: 1·2–1·5 m (4–5 ft)
A delightful rose with grey leaves (purple when young) and 40 mm (1½ inch) wide pink flowers during June. Space 600 mm (2 ft) apart.

Q

When is the best time to prune floribunda and hybrid tea roses, and how should this be done?

A

Hybrid tea types are pruned much more severely than floribunda forms. Both, by the way, are best pruned in early spring, before buds lengthen and are easily broken. Hybrid teas are pruned to encourage new shoots to develop from around the plant's base. Cut back the previous year's shoots to two or three buds of the older wood. Floribunda types are pruned less severely; the previous year's shoots should be cut back to six or seven buds of the older wood. On both types, cut out dead and crossing wood.

Q

Please suggest a climbing rose for a large south-facing wall and another attractive climber that will happily co-habit with it.

A

The rose *Rosa* 'Helen Knight', which has clear, yellow, saucer-shaped flowers 50 mm (2 inches) wide with slightly fern-like foliage, is a delight during June and July. It flowers at the same time as the Mountain Clematis (*Clematis montana*), which displays greyish-green leaves and almond-scented, white flowers with yellow stamens.

Q

I want to cover my pergola with a scented climbing rose. What varieties do you suggest?

A

There are several to choose from, including 'Gloire de Dijon', rising to 3·5–4·5 m (12–15 ft) with apricot and pink May flowers. 'Golden Showers' grows up to 2·4 m (8 ft) and is superb as a pillar rose, displaying pale gold flowers throughout summer and autumn, while 'Guinée' at 2·4–3 m (8–10 ft) with dark velvety-scarlet flowers, shaded black, flowers almost continuously. 'Madame Gregoire Staechelin' is a little more vigorous, rising to 4·5–6 m (15–20 ft) and is ideal for a north-facing situation; it bears double flowers shaded crimson.

PRUNING ROSES

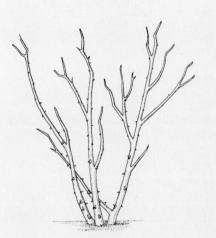

Hybrid tea *roses are pruned hard back to encourage new shoots to grow from the base of the plant. Always cut the shoots back to outward-pointing buds, to ensure good circulation of air within the plant. Cut back only into wood produced the previous year which still has dormant buds.*

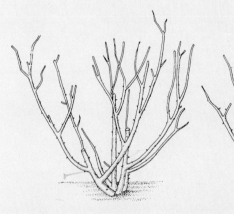

Floribunda *roses are not pruned as severely as hybrid-teas. Cut to outward pointing buds.*

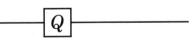

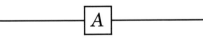

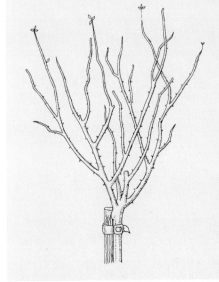

Standard *roses are pruned by cutting back shoots produced the previous year to outward pointing buds. Choose a mild spell in late February or early March.*

CLIMBERS & TRAILERS

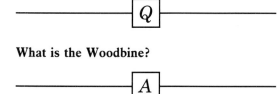

Q

What is the Woodbine?

A

Below *Flowers of the Woodbine or Early Dutch Honeysuckle (Lonicera periclymenum 'Belgica') are fragrant as well as colourful.*

This is the common name for *Lonicera periclymenum*, also known as Honeysuckle, a climber that grows to 6m (20ft) high, with terminal whorls of flowers from July to August. 'Belgica', the Early Dutch Honeysuckle, displays purple-red and yellow flowers during May and June; 'Serotina', the Late Dutch Honeysuckle, has red-purple flowers from July to October.

Q

I have a large blank wall I would like to cover with a handsome-leaved climber, ideally one with variegated leaves. What do you suggest?

A

There are several in which the leaf's green area is attractively blotched, mottled or rimmed with silver, white, pink or gold. Take your pick from *Actinidia kolomikta*, a tricoloured beauty with green leaves tipped white and pink; *Lonicera japonica* 'Aureo-reticulata', whose leaves are netted with striking yellow veins; *Trachelospermum jasminoides* 'Variegatum', in which they are edged and splashed with white; *Hedera* 'Goldheart', green, centrally splashed with gold; *Hedera colchica* 'Dentata Variegata', rimmed with creamy white.

Q

Can you tell me why my Passion Flower has not produced new shoots this spring?

A

Passiflora caerulea is not fully hardy in all areas and, to be reliable, needs a south or west-facing wall in the South or West of the country. Cold and especially wet soil during severe winters cause death to the plant. If you are in a cold area replant with a variegated ivy.

Q

I have a trellis on a warm wall near to my back door and would like to plant a scented climber. What do you suggest?

A

The Common White Jasmine, *Jasminum officinale*, is vigorous, often rising to 7·5 m (25 ft), and displays clusters of pure white flowers from June to October.

Abeliophyllum distichum, with its star-shaped, white flowers in late winter, is a delight. It is a deciduous shrub, growing only to 900 mm (3 ft) high, with the flowers borne on bare stems.

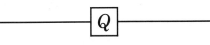

My neighbour's garage is an eye-sore. Is there a climber that would quickly camouflage it?

The fastest-growing climber is the Mile-a-Minute *Fallopia baldschuanicum* (better known as *Polygonum baldschuanicum*). It is also known as the Russian Vine. From July to October it displays masses of frothy-headed white flowers. It often grows 3–4·5 m (10–15 ft) a year, ultimately to a height of 10·5–12 m (35–40 ft) although unless given a tree to climb in, it seldom reaches this height, tending to spread sideways instead.

I have a cold, north-facing garage that I want to brighten up. How do you suggest I do this?

Several wall shrubs are suitable, such as the Firethorn *Pyracantha* × 'Orange Glow', *Cotoneaster horizontalis* and Flowering Quince (chaenomeles). Climbers to choose from include the Winter-flowering Jasmine (*Jasminum nudiflorum*) and the Climbing Hydrangea (*Hydrangea petiolaris*). Many members of the ivy (hedera) family are tough enough to be used.

The small-leaved types are better if a path is close to the garage, as the large-leaved types spread out considerably.

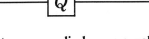

I would like to grow a climber up a wall which is three storeys high and would appreciate advice on the choice available.

You need a self-clinging climber for an area of that size, as it would be difficult to erect a trellis or wires over it. A suitable vigorous climber is *Parthenocissus quinquefolia*, the true Virginia Creeper. It is more or less self-clinging and reaches 12–18 m (40–60 ft) high, revealing leaves which turn brilliant crimson in autumn.

Slightly less vigorous, *Parthenocissus tricuspidata* at 9–12 m (30–40 ft) is the Boston Ivy with rich scarlet and crimson autumn leaves.

The Chinese Virginia Creeper (*Parthenocissus henryana*) rises to 7·5 m (25 ft) and displays brilliant red leaves in autumn.

Many of the ivies (hedera) are also suitable. The golden variegated types, such as large-leaved *Hedera colchica* 'Dentata Aurea', although more attractive than the all-green ones, are slightly slower growing.

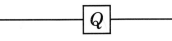

Can you suggest climbers with handsome leaves to cover my trelliswork? They must create a dense, peep-proof screen.

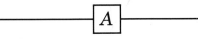

Humulus lupulus 'Aureus', the golden-leaved form of the hop, is superb for this position. It is a herbaceous climber and each year develops a fresh screen of three to five-lobed, soft-yellow leaves. When grown over trelliswork it soon develops a complete overhead canopy of leaves.

Another suitable climber is *Actinidia kolomikta*, whose leaves open green then assume cream and pink variegation. It is a robust climber and needs plenty of room.

Evergreens to suit your purpose include Canary Island Ivy (*Hedera canariensis* 'Variegata') also known as Gloire de Marengo, whose olive-green leaves are fetchingly edged with silver and cream, and *Trachelospermum jasminoides*, which, in addition to its richly scented, white flowers, has narrowly oval, polished green leaves. Many of the Honeysuckles, such as the Early and Late Dutch forms, will create a dense screen at eye-height, but often become bare of foliage at their bases.

Left *The Chinese Virginia Creeper* (Parthenocissus henryana), *a self-clinging climber prized for its autumn coloration.*

SOIL TYPES

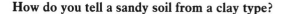

How do you tell a sandy soil from a clay type?

This is easily done by taking a handful of soil and rubbing it between your thumb and fore-finger, If, as it passes between these fingers, it produces a smooth, shiny surface you can be sure that the soil holds more clay than sand. If, however, the surface is pitted and rough the sample contains more sand than clay. In practice you will be able to identify clay soils easily by their stickiness and difficulty to cultivate. Clay soils retain plant foods better than light soils, but because they are wet and cold they will not produce early crops.

Can I improve heavy clay soil which is sticky in winter and dries out in lumps in summer?

Improve it by forking in all the rotted organic manure or garden compost you can muster, and sprinkling it with 100 g (4 oz) per sq. yd. of ground lime or gypsum each autumn. But don't add the manure and lime together, or there may be chemical reaction and a loss of valuable nitrogen from the soil.

It would also pay to top-dress (i.e. sprinkle the surface of) the soil with a seaweed soil con-ditioner, which physically splits up the sticky clay 'plates'. Repeat this treatment annually.

SHRUBS FOR DRY SOIL

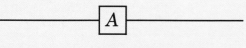

Please suggest a few shrubs which will grow well in dry soil in full sun.

Take your pick from the following selection:
Caryopterris × clandonensis **'Kew Blue'**: deep blue flowers from August to October; reaches 1 m (3 ft) in height.
Cistus × crispus **'Sunset'**: cerise flowers July to October; 750 mm (2½ ft) high and wide.
Cytisus praecox **'Allgold'**: deep yellow flowers on arching sprays in May; grows 1.5 m (5 ft) high and wide.
Genista lydia: wiry, arching green stems massed with tiny, butter-yellow flowers from May to June; 750 mm (2½ ft) high and wide.
Hebe **'Midsummer Beauty'**: lavender-purple flowers in tapering spires, July to August; 1.2 m (4 ft) high.
Hypericum patulum **'Hidcote'**: golden yellow, saucer-shaped flowers from June to September; 1.5 m (5 ft) high.
Phlomis fruticosa: Bright yellow flowers borne in tiered clusters round the stems, from June to July; 750 mm (2½ ft) high.
Salvia officinalis **'Icterina'**: handsome greyish green and yellow variegated leaves; 600 mm

(2 ft) high. Makes a spreading bush.
Santolina virens: hummocks of bright green, thread-like foliage; lemon-yellow flowers in summer; 450 mm (1½ ft) high.
Senecio **'Sunshine'** (formerly greyi): valued for its silvery-grey leaves and yellow flowers in summer: 900 mm (3 ft) high.
Spartium junceum: honey-scented, golden-yellow flowers borne freely on grass-like stems July to September; 2.5 m (8 ft) high.

Right Hebe *'Midsummer Beauty'*, *a pretty shrub for a dry, sunny position.*

Are there any flowering shrubs that will thrive in acid soil?

Enkianthus campanulatus
  Height: 2·1–2·4 m (7–8 ft)
  Spread: 1·8–2·1 m (6–7 ft)
A hardy, deciduous shrub with leaves that turn brilliant red in autumn, and which displays bell-shaped, creamy-yellow flowers with red veins during late spring and early summer.

Fothergilla monticola
  Height: 1·8–2·4 m (6–8 ft)
  Spread: 1·5–2·1 m (5–7 ft)
A hardy, deciduous shrub, with good autumn foliage in shades of orange and red, and sweetly-scented, creamy-white flowers that closely resemble small bottle-brushes.

Calico Bush (*Kalmia latifolia*)
  Height: 1·8–2·4 m (6–8 ft)
  Spread: 1·8–2·1 m (6–7 ft)
A hardy, evergreen shrub, with leathery leaves and 75–100 mm (3–4 inch) wide clusters of small, bright pink flowers during June.

Common Camellia (*Camellia japonica*)
  Height: 1·8–3 m (6–10 ft)
  Spread: 1·8–2·4 m (6–8 ft)
This is the well-known evergreen shrub that bears 75–130 mm (3–5 inch) wide flowers in colours from white to red and purple in late winter and spring. Many named forms are available in a range of flower shapes.

My soil is light, sandy, and well drained. Which bulbs would do well there?

There are several to choose from, including pink to white *Crinum × powellii*, flowering from July to September; Star of Bethlehem (*Ornithogalum umbellatum*), a carpeter for lightly shaded spots with branching heads of starry white blooms in May; Harlequin Flower (*Sparaxis tricolor*), valued for its small branching stems topped with red, yellow, purple and white blooms from May to June; and the Peacock Flower (*Tigridia pavonia*), magnificent with yellow, pink or white three-petalled blooms with distinctive centres.

COLOUR ALL YEAR ROUND

JAPANESE CHERRIES FOR SPRING COLOUR

Prunus 'Fugenzo': Double rose-pink flowers in drooping clusters.
Prunus 'Hokusai': Semi-double pale-pink flowers.
Prunus 'Ichiyo': Double shell-pink flowers, frilled at their edges in long-stalked clusters.
Prunus 'Jo-nioi': Beautifully scented white flowers.
Prunus 'Ojochin': Pale pink flowers in long-stalked clusters.

Below *The autumn-flowering bulb* Nerine bowdenii *makes a delightful show.*

I find bulbs very reliable in my garden. Please suggest some for late summer and autumn colour.

There is a wide range to choose from, including *Acidanthera bicolor*, which is hardy outside only in the mildest climates and which displays fragrant, star-shaped flowers during August and September. *Amaryllis belladonna* is another tender bulb, with 100–130 mm (4–5 inch) wide, trumpet-shaped, pale pink flowers during September and October.

Colchicum autumnale is easy to grow and displays white or rose-pink flowers during autumn. *Nerine bowdenii* has 100–150 mm (4–6 inch) wide heads of pink flowers from September to November, and *Sternbergia lutea* displays 50 mm (2 inch) long, shining yellow flowers during September and October.

I have a garden pond in an informal setting and want to plant shrubs around it that have coloured stems in winter. Please suggest some plants for this purpose.

Many of the Dogwoods are suitable, such as *Cornus alba* with mid-green leaves turning orange and red in autumn, followed by beautiful deep red stems during winter. *Cornus alba* 'Westonbirt' has brilliant sealing wax red stems in winter, while 'Sibirica' reveals crimson shoots. For yellow shoots choose *Salix alba* 'Vitellina', and for bright orange shoots try *Salix alba* 'Chermesina'.

My garden is usually bare of colour in winter. Please suggest trees which have colourful bark during this dull season.

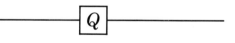

Some of the best known ones include:
Paperbark Maple (*Acer griseum*)
   Height: 3–4·5 m (10–15 ft)
   Spread: 1·8–2·4 m (6–8 ft)
Orange-brown old bark peeling to reveal cinnamon-coloured new bark.
Snake-bark Maple/Mousewood (*Acer pensylvanicum*)
   Height: 5·4–6 m (18–20 ft)
   Spread: 3–3·5 m (10–12 ft)
Bark develops silvery-white stripes.
White-barked Himalayan Birch (*Betula jacquemontii*)
   Height: 6–7·5 m (20–25 ft)
   Spread: 4·5–5·4 m (15–18 ft)
Superb birch, with beautiful white peeling bark.
Himalayan Birch (*Betula utilis*)
   Height: 6–7·5 m (20–25 ft)
   Spread: 4·5–5·4 m (15–18 ft)
Magnificent grey-white bark which contrasts with the peeling cinnamon-brown branches.
Prunus serrula
   Height: 6–7·5 m (20–25 ft)
   Spread: 4·5–5·4 m (15–18 ft)
Beautiful shiny bark, which peels in strips to reveal reddish-brown bark beneath.

Q

I want to plant a tree with colourful fruits during autumn and into early winter. Have you any suggestions?

A

Malus 'Golden Hornet' is certainly one of the best types you could choose, with masses of bright yellow, almost conical fruits that persist into December. It is a medium-sized tree, rising to 4·5–5·4 m (15–18 ft) with a spread of 3–4·5 m (10–15 ft).

Malus 'Red Sentinel' has glossy, bright red fruits that persist even longer, into early spring. It is slightly smaller, with a height of 3–4·5 m (10–15 ft) and width of 2·4–3·5 m (8–12 ft).

Many sorbus species produce superb fruits, such as *S. aucuparia* 'Sheerwater Seedling' with spectacular orange-red berries, *S. aucuparia* 'Xanthocarpa' with bright yellow berries, and *S.* 'Embley' with magnificent, glistening, orange-red berries. And for small, rosy-red berries that turn first pink then blush white, choose the dainty *Sorbus vilmorinii*.

Q

One of my greatest joys is watching spring arrive in the garden. I have plenty of spring bulbs and now wish to plant a spring-flowering tree to harmonize with them. What do you recommend?

A

Some of the best spring trees are the flowering cherries. Perhaps *Prunus subhirtella* 'Pendula Rosea', the weeping spring cherry, is one of the best known early-flowering ornamental trees. It displays a mushroom-habit with flowers rich pink in bud, opening to pinkish-white. The weeping branches tend to fuse with daffodils planted underneath.

For a very small garden Cheal's Weeping Cherry, with a height of 4·5–6 m (15–20 ft) and spread of 4·5–5·4 m (15–18 ft) is superb. The arching and pendulous branches bear double pink flowers in March or April.

Even smaller is *Prunus triloba* with a height and spread of 3–3·5 m (10–12 ft) and 25 mm (1 inch) wide, clear pink flowers during late March and into April.

Right *A stunning display of spring colour.*

THE DIFFICULT GARDEN

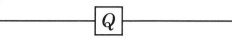

Each year a neighbouring tree gets larger and casts more shade over an area of my garden. Please suggest a few evergreen shrubs that I can grow there.

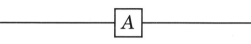

Below Pachysandra terminalis *'Variegata', an attractive evergreen shrub which does well in shade.*

You could choose from any of the following, although eventually the site may be so dark that you will have to discuss the tree's removal with your neighbour.

Arctostaphylos uva-ursi: creeping shrub with white, pink-tinged flowers.
Aucuba japonica: valued for its evergreen, often golden-speckled, leaves and red fruits.
Common Box (Buxus sempervirens): neat evergreen leaves and an ability to thrive in quite gloomy places.
Elaeagnus, especially *E.* × *ebbingei*: fast growing with silvery undersides to the leaves.
Fatsia japonica: white bobble flowers in winter and handsome fingered leaves.
Oregon Grape (Mahonia aquifolium): golden yellow flowers followed by clusters of blue-black, grape-like fruits.
Pachysandra terminalis: creeping carpeter a few inches high with leaves clustered at stem ends. *P. terminalis* 'Variegata' is the most distinctive form.
Sarcococca confusa: very fragrant small white flowers in winter, evergreen leaves.
Skimmia japonica **'Foremanii'**: white flowers in summer followed by abundance of scarlet fruits.
Snowberry (Symphoricarpos): pinkish-white, urn-shaped flowers give rise to polystyrene-textured white or purple-pink berries.
Vaccinium vitis-idae: good carpeter with white tinged-pink flowers followed by red fruit.

Each autumn, be sure to remove fallen leaves from on top of these plants, especially the lower-growing types.

Can you suggest a tree I could plant as a focal point from my kitchen window? The soil is poor – infilling deposited by the builders.

Several trees could do well there, and become established quickly. These include *Acer platanoides* 'Drummondii', with its white-edged leaves, *Acer pseudoplatanus* 'Worlei' with yellow leaves from spring until mid-summer, and *Betula pendula*, the beautiful Silver Birch, so useful when planting in a grouping. This tree looks especially effective in a lawn setting with small crocuses growing around it. The silver bark is a further attraction, looking particularly dramatic in winter.

The Swedish cut-leaved birch, *Betula dalecarlica*, is an especially attractive form, with pendulous branches down to soil-level. It also has attractive bark.

PLANTS FOR THE COAST

Q

We have just retired to the coast, and the few plants we took with us are being scorched by the salt spray in the wind. What plants do you suggest we try?

A

The first job is to establish a salt-resistant screen around your garden. For this purpose, try the conifers x *Cupressocyparis leylandii*, *Cupressus macrocarpa* or *Cupressus arizonica*, all of which are useful for shelterbelts.

Behind this screen shrubs can be planted, such as *Elaeagnus ebbingei*, pink or red-flowered escallonia, orange-berried *Hippophae rhamnoides* (the Sea Buckthorn), molten gold flowered *Ulex europaeus* (Gorse), silver-tasselled *Garrya elliptica* and white flowered, red, orange or yellow-berried pyracantha.

There are, of course, many others such as pink-flowered, feathery-leaved *Tamarix gallica*; white-flowered *Hebe brachysiphon*; and *Euonymus japonicus*, a glossy, leathery-leaved stalwart that happily takes a salty battering.

Right Pyracantha atalantioides 'Aurea'.

Q

I live in a town and my front garden often suffers damage as it is next to a main thoroughfare. Are there any shrubs that have natural defences against ill-use?

A

What you need are prickly plants. There are several to choose from, including coral-red berried *Berberis* × *rubrostilla* (deciduous), orange-flowered *Berberis* × *stenophylla* (evergreen), pink, red or white-flowered chaenomeles (deciduous) or *Elaeagnus angustifolia* (deciduous). You could also try orange-fruited *Hippophae rhamnoides* (deciduous), double golden yellow *Ulex europaeus* 'Plenus' (evergreen) or yucca (evergreen), a beauty with an impressive spire of white lily-like flowers. Pernettya is a very hardy evergreen and soon forms a dense wiry thicket. *Pernettya mucronata* 'Alba' produces clusters of white fruits.

Q

The traffic on the road outside my house has increased considerably in recent years, with the ensuing noise reaching a near intolerable level. Are hedges any use in reducing noise?

A

Yes, they can be of great help. Evergreen coniferous hedges are best for absorbing the noise. If the size of your garden allows it, set the plants in two rows, either making a very thick single hedge or two rows several feet apart. The rapid-growing x *Cupressocyparis leylandii* is often too large, but *Thuya plicata* planted 600–750 mm (2–2½ ft) apart makes a good screen for small gardens.

An alternative method is to use the combination of a wooden fence (up to 1·8 m (6 ft)) with a line of conifers behind it. Plant the conifers about 900 mm (3 ft) away from the fence to leave plenty of space for their development.

CONIFERS FOR WET GARDENS

The Swamp Cypress or Bald Cypress (*Taxodium distichum*) does well in wet soils or those that are permanently moist. Grows 7·5–10·5 m (25–35 ft) high, and is ideal as a specimen on a wet lawn.

The Dawn Redwood (*Metasequoia glyptostroboides*) rises to 9–13·5 m (30–45 ft) and is ideal for planting in a group at the side of a large pond.

The Sitka Spruce (*Picea sitchensis*) is larger and grows up to 18 m (60 ft) and is best featured as a specimen conifer in a large, wet lawn.

THE INSTANT GARDEN

Above *Stone troughs or sinks are ideal for a small collection of rock garden plants.*

Androsace lanuginosa 'Leichtlinii,' with trailing silver stems and white, pink-eyed flowers; *Draba bryoides*, a green cushion of leaves dotted with golden flowers on thread-like stems; *Gentiana verna*, with starry, rich blue flowers; *Micromeria corsica*, aromatic thorny clusters with rosy lavender flowers, and *Sempervivum arachnoideum*, leaf rosettes covered with 'spiders' webs.

Please recommend some long flowering plants for a hanging basket that will be in full sun.

Create a display to remember with cascading fuchsias, such as deep red 'Marinka', white flushed carmine 'Lillibet', white, carmine and red 'Cascade' red and white 'Swingtime'.

Interplant with ivy-leaved pelargoniums. Some of the finest are double mauve and maroon 'La France', white-flowered, cream-edged leaved 'L'Elegante', bright double pink 'Madame Crousse' and crimson 'Sir Percy Blakeney. Trailing lobelia in white, light or deep blue and red looks well among both fuchsias and pelargoniums.

All flower throughout summer and early autumn, only ceasing when chilly nights start in mid-October. The compost must be watered every day during the height of summer. Once a week give a liquid feed with this watering.

I have an old stone sink. How should I prepare it for planting a few small rock garden plants?

First, check that the drainage hole is free and open. To enable you to see the plants in the container more clearly place the sink – before it is filled – on a firm-based slab of rock or some other solid support. Then, place a piece of perforated zinc over the drainage hole and cover the base of the sink with broken pieces of pots or stones. Place a layer of moistened peat over the stones, then top up with a loam-based compost to within 12 mm (½ inch) of the rim. This allows for settlement of the compost. Small rocks can be placed on the compost to create the look of a natural miniature rock garden. Washed gravel sprinkled over the surface after the plants have been set in position adds the finishing touch and helps to produce an effective setting.

Plants suitable for stone sinks include

Can I stand a window-box directly on a ledge, or should I fix brackets to the wall?

Assuming that the window-ledge is flat and strong enough to support the box – which will be heavy when filled with compost and subsequently watered – it is all right to put the box there if the window is a sash-type. Casement windows that open outwards would obviously be obstructed by the box. In this case, brackets would have to be fixed to the wall, about 45 cm (1½ ft) below the window. Remember that water will drip out of the window-box, and will stain a coloured-painted wall. A plastic drip tray under the box will prevent water running down the wall.

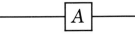

I have access to a small roof-top garden. Is it possible to grow plants there?

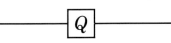

It is, but do check that it has a strong base, you have permission to use it, and that excess water is able to drain away easily. Because roof tops are usually buffeted by wind, ensure that the containers have firm bases. Use large tubs, which often look best when set in a small group.

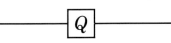

I have a large round clay pot that I want to plant for a summer display. Is it better to have one large plant, with others set around it, or a glorious mixture?

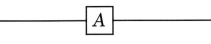

If it is an attractive pot that would be highlighted by a large plant, you could use a fuchsia as a central theme, with pink or white petunias, white alyssum, 'Cambridge-blue' trailing lobelia and cascading pink, red or white Ivy-leaved geraniums around the edges.

Above *Select container plants so that some give height and others cascade over the edges of the tub when in full bloom. Flowers planted near the base provide an attractive 'frame'.*

HANGING BASKETS

This year I want to have a hanging basket in flower early in summer. What should I do?

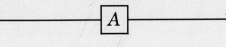

The key is to have ready for planting a good selection of half-hardy annuals, such as lobelia and petunia, and half-hardy perennials, such as ivy-leaved geraniums and pendant fuchsias.

When planting the basket, ideally use a compressed peat 'insert', or black or green polythene slit at the base for drainage, and set a deepish tray at the bottom to act as a reservoir in dry spells. Use loam-based rather than peat-based compost as the former holds water better in windy weather. Trailers, such as lobelia, ivy-leaved geraniums and helichrysum can be planted through the sides of a wire basket.

Keep the basket in a greenhouse or conservatory until mid to late May when nights have lost their chilly 'bite'. Then position it in full sun and water freely.

THE ROCK GARDEN

Above Erinus alpinus, *an ideal plant for rock gardens and dry walls.*

ROCK GARDEN SHRUBS
Garland Flower (*Daphne cneorum*)
   Height: 300 mm (1 ft)
   Spread: 600 mm (2 ft)
Carpeting evergreen with neat, small leaves interspersed in May and June with clusters of richly scented, rose-pink flowers.
Rock Rose (*Helianthemum nummularium*)
   Height: 150–200 mm (6–8 inches)
   Spread: 600–900 mm (2–3 ft)
Ground-hugging evergreen ideal for sprawling over outcrops. Massed display of 15–25 mm (½–1 inch) wide, saucer-shaped flowers in many hues during May and June.
***Spiraea nipponica* 'Snowmound'**
   Height: 300 mm (1 ft)
   Spread: 600 mm (2 ft)
Enchanting hummocks of green foliage dotted with white, green-centred flowers in June.

My garden is small, without a slope. Is it still possible to grow rock garden plants?

The essential elements for a successful rock garden are an open site, preferably facing south or west, no trees which will cast their leaves over the plants in autumn, and good drainage. Even without the benefit of a slope, rock garden plants can still be grown in a raised bed. Use plenty of clean rubble to form a freely-draining base, placing weed-free soil over this. Pieces of natural stone can be positioned in the soil to appear like natural rock outcrops. The natural rock strata should be aligned at all times.

Q

I have a dry stone wall. Which plants would thrive there to provide early summer colour?

A

There are several to choose from, including:
***Aethionema* × 'Warley Rose'**
   Height: 100–150 mm (4–6 inches)
   Spread: 300–380 mm (12–15 inches)
A beautiful hybrid with narrow, grey-green leaves and 50–75 mm (2–3 inch) long spike of deep rose flowers during spring.
Arenaria montana
   Height: 100–150 mm (4–6 inches)
   Spread: 380–450 mm (15–18 inches)
Glistening, white, saucer-shaped flowers amid mid- to dark-green leaves in early summer.
Asperula lilaciflora caespitosa
   Height: 50–75 mm (2–3 inches)
   Spread: 100–150 mm (4–6 inches)
A neat carpeter, with deep carmine, tubular flowers during early summer.
Erinus alpinus
   Height: 75 mm (3 inches)
   Spread: 130–150 mm (5–6 inches)
A low, tufted plant with bright pink, star-shaped flowers from spring to late summer.
Geranium cinereum subcaulescens
   Height: 100–150 mm (4–6 inches)
   Spread: 300–380 mm (12–15 inches)
An alpine geranium with crimson-magenta 25 mm (1 inch) wide flowers in early summer.

YELLOW DISPLAY

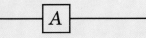

Can you suggest a small, yellow-flowered shrub for the top of my rock garden?

Left Cytisus x kewensis, *an excellent rock garden shrub, which displays masses of creamy-yellow flowers.*

There are several members of the broom family to choose from, but the one perhaps best suited to a small rock garden is *Cytisus × kewensis* at 300–600 mm (1–2 ft) high and 750–900 mm (2½–3 ft) wide. During May it develops a stunning array of pea-shaped, pale yellow flowers. Other choices include *Genista pilosa*, 450 mm (1½ ft) high and 600–750 mm (2–2½ ft) wide. During May and June it produces a mass of small, yellow, pea-like flowers amid tangled shoots. The form 'Prostrata' is often grown, and this seldom rises above 75–100 mm (3–4 inches) with a spread up to 1·2 m (4 ft).

Genista sagittalis, 100–150 mm (4–6 inches) high and 450–600 mm (1½–2 ft) wide, is an interesting miniature broom, now correctly known as *Chamaespartium sagittale*, but seldom listed under this name. The small, yellow, pea-like flowers appear in summer. It is a good ground cover shrub, or for trailing and scrambling over rocks.

Can you recommend an upright water plant with flowers and variegated foliage for the edge of my pond?

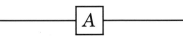

You could not do better than *Iris laevigata* 'Variegata'. It grows to 450–600 mm (1½–2 ft) high, with a spread of 250–380 mm (10–15 inches). Position it in water up to 150 mm (6 inches) deep, or in moist soil at the pond's edges. Its upright, sword-like, stiff leaves display silver-striped, vertical bands. Soft-blue, iris-like flowers are borne at the tops of stems during early June. Other suitable plants include:

Iris pseudacorus
   Height: 900 mm–1·2 m (3–4 ft)
   Spread: 450–600 mm (1½–2 ft)
A hardy water iris, suitable for water depths up to 380 mm (15 inches), with upright, sword-like, blue-green leaves. Yellow, iris-like, flowers are borne five or more at the tops of stems during early June. A variegated form is also available.
Scirpus tabernaemontanus 'Zebrinus'
   Height: 300–750 mm (1–2½ ft)
   Spread: 300–380 mm (12–15 inches)

An eye-catching, herbaceous perennial, ideal for water up to 150 mm (6 inches) deep. Its tubular, upright leaves are banded white and green, somewhat resembling porcupine quills.

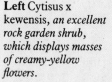

I have inherited a pile of sandstone and Westmorland limestone in my new garden. I intend to form two rock gardens. Any tips on using the stone would be welcome.

The sandstone should always be laid with the strata (the layers which form the stone) arranged horizontally. Position the individual pieces so that they either butt up to one another or overlap slightly. This helps to prevent soil erosion. They can then be formed into a series of terraces.

The Westmorland limestone, however, is more difficult to use, and should be laid with the largest surface area to the ground. Position the pieces to form a series of irregular small terraces. They are fitted together like a jig-saw puzzle, with as little space as possible between the joins. Small, low-growing plants can then be planted between them.

THE FLOWER ARRANGER'S GARDEN

BULBS FOR CUT FLOWERS

Acidanthera bicolor **'Murielae'**: scented, white, purple-centred, starry flowers in August.

Daffodils (*Narcissus*): especially fine are the scented bunch-flowered varieties such as white, yellow-centred 'Grand Primo Citroniere', 'Paper White Grandiflora' and golden 'Grand Soleil d'Or'.

Gladiolus: spikes of red, pink, blue, orange, yellow trumpet blooms from July to September.
Harlequin flower (Sparaxis): choice combinations of flower colours: pink, red, orange and white with contrasting bronzy red or yellow centres.

Iris: Dutch and Spanish hybrids in white, yellow, blue and purple and English hybrids in white, blue, pink or purple, June to July.

Lilium: Mid-Century Hybrids, especially lemon-yellow 'Destiny' and nasturtium-red 'Enchantment'.

Tulips (*Tulipa*): scented varieties such as golden 'Bellona' and golden orange 'De Wet' and the long lasting, soft orange and purple-flame 'Princess Irene' bring colour to early spring.

Right Cosmos bipannatus (Cosmea) *'Gloria', a good flower for cutting and arranging.*

I am an avid flower arranger and would appreciate your suggestions for flowers suitable for cutting and displaying in the home.

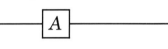

There are many that produce superb flowers and last a long time when cut. The list below gives a selection of hardy annuals which make attractive arrangements.

Love-lies-bleeding (*Amaranthus caudatus*)
'Crimson' and 'Viridis' are varieties prized for their scarlet and green pendant tassels; both grow to a height of 750 mm (2½ ft).

Pot Marigold/English Marigold (*Calendula officinalis*)
'Orange Gitana'. Superb, compact plant with

fully double orange blooms, 300 mm (1 ft) high.

Clarkia (*Clarkia elegans*)
'Brilliant Mixture' comes in soft hues of salmon, scarlet, purple and orange and white; 600 mm (2 ft) high.

Coreopsis (*Calliopsis*)
'Dwarf Mixed' produces an abundance of golden-yellow, maroon or crimson flowers, 300 mm (1 ft) high.

Cosmos (*Cosmos bipinnatus (Cosmea)*)
'Gloria'. Valued for its very large, rose-pink blooms, up to 900 mm (3 ft) high.

Godetia grandiflora **'Sybil Sherwood'**, in salmon-pink or orange with a white rim, grows just 300 mm (1 ft) high.

Love-in-a-mist (*Nigella damascena*)
'Persian Jewels', white, pink, rose-red, mauve and purple, 450 mm (18 inches) high.

Black-eyed Susan (*Rudbeckia hirta*)
'Goldilocks'. Double and semi-double, rich golden-yellow flowers contrasting with central black cone. Branches freely, 450–600 mm (1½–2 ft) high. (Also known as Coneflower.)

Sweet Scabious (*Scabiosa atropurpurea*)
'Paper Moon'. Lavender flowers give way to intriguing papery spheres of blue-centred miniature shuttlecocks, 900 mm (3 ft) high.

Zinnia elegans (Half-hardy annual)
Chartreuse-green 'Envy' has superb semi-double and double blooms, 500 mm (20 inches).

My neighbour has some very decorative silvery and feathery plumes at the tops of long, stiff stems. What are they?

This is the Pampas Grass (*Cortaderia selloana*) from Argentina. It is a member of the grass family, best planted as a specimen at the edge of an informal pond or in a lawn. It grows 1·8–2·7 m (6–9 ft) high and forms a clump 1·5–1·8 m (5–6 ft) wide. The long stems can be cut off in autumn and placed in a large, firmly-based container on the floor. The plume-like heads dry and last a long time.

Incidentally, Pampas Grass looks magnificent during winter when covered with frost and with low winter light falling on the plumes. For this reason set it in an open position, which is not continually shaded.

Left *Love-in-a-Mist*
(Nigella damascena
*'Persian Jewels') looks
stunning both in the
garden and the home.*

$$Q$$

I have a border of herbaceous perennials for cutting, and would now like to grow a few shrubs that will provide foliage for background colour. What do you suggest?

$$A$$

There are several to choose from, such as *Lonicera nitida* 'Baggesen's Gold' with small, golden-coloured leaves, *Philadelphus coronarius* 'Aureus' with soft yellow leaves, and the golden privet, again with gold leaves. For silver foliage *Artemesia arborescens* is superb, and *Eucalyptus gunnii* has blue-tinged silvery foliage. For really stunning, dark plum-purple foliage choose *Cotinus coggygria* 'Foliis Purpureis'. *Cotinus coggygria* 'Royal Red' is equally fine.

ORNAMENTAL GRASSES FOR CUTTING FOR HOME DECORATION

HARDY ANNUAL GRASSES
Pearl Grass (Briza maxima)
    Height: 450 mm (1½ ft)
    Spread: 300 mm (1 ft)
Long, nodding spikes of green and white flowers.
Hordeum jubatum
    Height: 450 mm (1½ ft)
    Spread: 300 mm (1 ft)
Long-haired, silky, barley-like tassels.
Lagurus ovatus
    Height: 450 mm (1½ ft)
    Spread: 300 mm (1 ft)
Woolly plumes borne on long stems.
Setaria italica
    Height: 450 mm (1½ ft)
    Spread: 300 mm (1 ft)
Nodding, large, graceful flower heads.

HERBACEOUS GRASSES
Pennisetum alopecuroides
    Height: 900 mm (3 ft)
    Spread: 450 mm (1½ ft)
A long-lived grass, with feathery, tawny-yellow plumes during September and October.
Pennisetum orientale
    Height: 300 mm (1 ft)
    Spread: 300 mm (1 ft)
Poker-like flower spires from July to October.
Stipa gigantea
    Height: 900 mm (3 ft)
    Spread: 450 mm (1½ ft)
Dense clumps of grey-green leaves.

$$Q$$

I am planning a herbaceous border. Please suggest a few plants that would provide flowers for cutting. And if any are suitable for drying, please indicate this.

$$A$$

The following plants will provide colour for the home: yellow-flowered *Achillea filipendulina* 'Gold Plate' (suitable for drying), pink, apricot and orange alstroemeria, white papery-flowered anaphalis (suitable for drying), primrose yellow, daisy-flowered anthemis, blue, red and pink aster, blue-flowered catananche (suitable for drying), pinkish-rose centaurea, blue delphinium, yellow doronicum, globe-headed blue echinops (suitable for drying), silvery-blue-flowered eryngium (suitable for drying), bronzy red helenium, blue-flowered limonium (suitable for drying), pink, scarlet or violet-purple monarda, pink, red or white phlox, pink physostegia, red and pink pyrethrum, golden rudbeckia, blue scabiosa, rose-pink solidago and golden-yellow trollius.

THE CHILDREN'S GARDEN

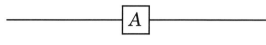

Q

Our children are just starting to make use of the garden, tottering out and examining the plants. Are there any plants that I should evict from the garden because they are poisonous?

A

There are many cultivated plants that children should avoid, as well as a wide number of native plants. Sometimes it is only certain parts of plants that are poisonous, and it is therefore wise to teach children not to pick and eat any leaves and fruits unless you are with them and can identify the plant as harmless.

The list of plants with parts that are poisonous is extensive and includes aconitum, anemones, aquilegias, arum, *Caltha palustris*, colchicum, *Convallaria majalis*, *Daphne mezereum*, delphinium, dicentra, *Digitalis purpurea*, *Eranthis hyemalis*, *Fritillaria meleagris*, helleborus, *Hyacinthus orientalis*, *Kalmia latifolia*, *Leycesteria formosa*, Common Privet, lupins, narcissus, *Ornithogalum umbellatum*, potato, Buttercups, rhubarb, *Robinia pseudoacacia*, Bluebells, tomatoes and mistletoe.

To ban all of these from a garden one would be near reduced to just a lawn!

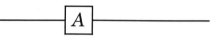

Q

Are there any 'dramatic' plants which would fascinate children?

A

There are several insectivorous plants which children love to watch. The Venus Fly-trap (*Dionaea muscipula*) has jaw-like leaves with large comb-like edges that snap together when a small insect walks into the jaws and triggers the mechanism that closes the entrance. It is quite a tolerant plant, needing a minimum water temperature of 10°C (50°F). In summer it can be placed in a sunny position. It needs plenty of water at all times.

Pitcher Plants (*Sarracenia*) are sometimes also known as Indian Cup, Side-saddle Flower and Trumpet Leaf. The funnel-shaped leaves contain a liquid that draws inquisitive insects. The insect's body is slowly dissolved in the liquid and the food value absorbed by the plant. They are too tender to be grown outside, needing the same temperature as the Venus Fly-trap.

Sundews (*Drosera*) have hairs that produce a sticky fluid that attracts insects and then digests them. Sundews are best treated in the same way as the Venus Fly-trap.

Right *The distinctive Golden Sunflower, whose huge bright blooms make it a favourite with children.*

FLOWERS FOR CHILDREN

Q

My children are now starting to take an interest in flowers. Please suggest some they can grow easily from seeds.

A

Perhaps the best known children's flower is the Sunflower (*Helianthus annuus*) that often rises to 3 m (10 ft) and bears 300 mm (1 ft) wide yellow flower heads. Seeds can be sown in spring where they are to flower. Snapdragons – or Bunny Rabbits – are another favourite. These are *Antirrhinum majus* and are usually sown early under glass. Children love to use the flowers for 'nipping' noses. Other fun plants are Nasturtiums (*Tropaeolum majus*), whose round leaves can be used as dolls' hats.

Is it possible to grow a Sensitive Plant without a greenhouse, as the leaves never fail to delight children?

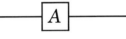

This plant, *Mimosa pudica*, also called the Humble Plant, is a tender shrub but is usually grown as an annual. Its leaves curl up when touched even lightly. It needs a minimum winter temperature of 18–21°C (64–70°F), and plenty of humidity. It is therefore best in a greenhouse.

Which popular houseplants would children find interesting?

The Spider Plant (*Chlorophytum comosum*) seldom fails to interest children, with its long and narrow variegated leaves. An added attraction is supplied by the miniature plants that appear at the ends of long stems.

A plant with a similar trait is Mother-of-Thousands (*Saxifraga stolonifera*). The round, mid-green leaves display silvery veins above, with undersurfaces flushed red. Small plants arise at the ends of thin runners. It is best positioned on a shelf, so that the runners can trail.

The Pick-a-back Plant (*Tolmiea menziesii*) produces mid-green, maple-like leaves on which small plantlets grow. It is also called Youth-on-Age and Thousand Mothers.

Above *Children are fascinated by the Sensitive Plant (*Mimosa pudica*), whose leaves curl up when touched. The leaves are at their most sensitive at a temperature of 24°C (75°F), although they will curl up at lower temperatures, but more slowly.*

FURTHER EASY FLOWERS FROM SEED

Mignonette (*Reseda odorata*)
   Height: 300–750 mm (1–2½ ft)
   Spread: 200–250 mm (8–10 inches)
A hardy annual with small yellow-white flowers that are borne from June to October.

Candytuft (*Iberis umbellata*)
   Height: 150–380 mm (6–15 inches)
   Spread: 150–230 mm (6–9 inches)
A hardy annual with clusters of white, red or purple flowers from June to September.

Love-in-a-Mist (*Nigella damascena*)
   Height: 450–600 mm (1½–2 ft)
   Spread: 200–300 mm (8–12 inches)
A hardy annual with bright green, fern-like foliage and cornflower-blue or white flowers from June to August.

Californian Poppy (*Eschscholzia californica*)
   Height: 300–380 mm (12–15 inches)
   Spread: 200–250 mm (8–10 inches)
A hardy annual with poppy-like, saucer-shaped orangey flowers from June to October.

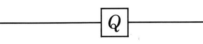

The grass beneath my children's garden swing has long since disappeared. Is there a more resilient grass I could try?

No grass is tough enough to put up with skidding and sliding under swings. Re-site the swing to a more verdant part of the lawn and re-sow or re-turf the bald patch. If re-sowing, fork the soil, sprinkle with balanced fertilizer, rake in and keep level and sow seeds of Suttons Summer Play at 40–50 g (1½–2 oz) per sq. yd. Make sure they are dressed with bird deterrent to keep the feathered fraternity away. If re-turfing, fork and level the site, feed as for sowing, and bond the turves so they knit together quickly. Brush soil over the cracks and water freely to stop edges curling.

If re-siting the swing isn't feasible, get a thick, rubber-based mat for the youngsters to land on.

RESTORING A NEGLECTED GARDEN

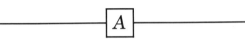

My new garden has plenty of trees and shrubs in it, but most of them are in the wrong positions. Is it possible to move some of the smaller ones, and how should I go about it?

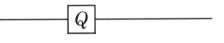

Large trees are certainly difficult for home gardeners to move successfully, so concentrate on changing the positions of small shrubs and conifers. If the plant is very small, dig completely around and under it, moving it with as much soil as possible. For larger ones, dig around the plant during one year, so that the sizeable cut roots will develop fine feeding ones. If the tree or shrub is tall and liable to catch the wind, support it with a stout stake or tie it securely in position with three guy lines. The following year dig it up completely and replant it. Placing the soil-ball on a piece of sacking will help to prevent the roots being damaged while it is being moved.

Evergreen plants are best moved when the soil is warm and the weather neither too cold nor too hot – late spring or early autumn is best. Deciduous plants are best moved in winter after their leaves have fallen.

Erecting a screen of hessian around evergreens to shelter them from the wind will reduce moisture loss from the leaves and speed recovery. Syringing the foliage with water also helps, as does coating the leaves with a plastic anti-transpirant spray.

We have just moved to a new garden which is choked with couch grass. What is the best way to get rid of it, and is it possible to use chemical sprays to eradicate it?

Weedkillers based on the herbicide dalapon or alloxydim sodium can be used, applied in a diluted form according to the manufacturer's instructions. However, although more strenuous, it is more effective to dig the entire garden to a foot or so deep – the depth of one spade – during winter. As you are digging the soil, remove *all* perennial weeds and burn them. It is difficult to extricate all pieces of perennial weeds, so during spring and summer keep the soil well cultivated to prevent them producing top-growth.

I have just taken over a neglected orchard of apples and pears. Many of the trees have branches that I will have to remove. Is there any special time or way of doing this?

Large branches are best removed during winter when leaves have fallen, the tree is dormant and it is easier to see what you are doing. First, cut off the branch 30–45 cm (1–1½ ft) from the trunk. The branch can then be cut off close to the trunk without any fear of the weight of the branch pulling it down and tearing the bark on the trunk. Pare the cut surface smooth with a sharp knife, then completely cover the wound with a fungicidal paint.

Below *Four steps to removing a branch. First, lop the branch 30–45 cm (1–1½ ft) from where it joins the trunk, then cut it off flush with the trunk. Pare the rough edges with a sharp knife, then completely cover the wound with a fungicidal paint.*

WEEDKILLERS

Q

The drive of our new house is peppered with weeds. They are too deep to dig out, and in any case this would damage the drive. Are there any chemicals that will control them?

A

There are available several 'total' weedkillers based on aminotriazole, MCPA, simazine, glyphosate and dicamba, but ensure that the chemicals do not come into contact with border flowers. A large piece of board can be held between the chemical and border to prevent spray drifting on to healthy plants.

Keep a special watering can or bucket for using herbicides, and wash all equipment thoroughly after use – including your hands.

Q

We have inherited a large laurel hedge at the bottom of our new garden. If we cut it back severely will it break into growth again?

A

The Common Laurel (*Prunus laurocerasus*) often reaches 6 m (20 ft), with a similar spread. It can be cut back in mild, frost-free weather in April or May. You may require saws as well as pruning secateurs to do this. The answer to the second part of your question is, yes; it is amazing how quickly the hedge will recover and produce attractive foliage.

Q

My new garden is continually wet during winter. How can I put a stop to this?

A

The best method of draining land is by tile drains, but it is an expensive method. However, if the drains are properly laid, they will last a long time. The process involves digging trenches 60–90 cm (2–3 ft) deep, in a herringbone fashion with a steady decline to a ditch or soakaway dug at the bottom of the slope.

An alternative and cheaper method is to use brick rubble. Dig out the trenches in the same way, but fill the bottom with 23 cm (9 inches) of brick rubble. Place a layer of inverted turves over the bricks to prevent soil becoming packed around them and stopping the flow of water.

HERRINGBONE DRAINAGE SYSTEM

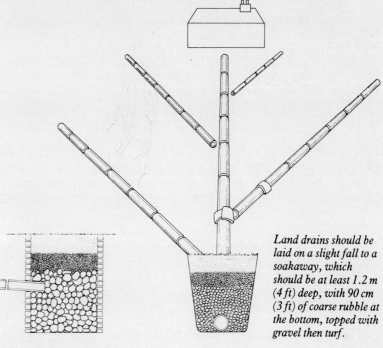

Land drains should be laid on a slight fall to a soakaway, which should be at least 1.2 m (4 ft) deep, with 90 cm (3 ft) of coarse rubble at the bottom, topped with gravel then turf.

PESTS & DISEASES

Q

My pansies appear to be dying from stems that are rotting. Have you any idea what could be causing this rot?

A

If your soil is heavy and wet, this could be the cause. These conditions tend to encourage soil-borne organisms to enter the stems at soil-level, causing the plant to rot. Remove the infected plants and all of their roots. Before planting fresh pansies sterilize the soil with Jeyes Fluid or Basamid and dust the holes with calomel.

Q

Many of my tulips – especially those newly emerging through the soil – are stunted and distorted. Some bulbs have foliage with yellowish streaks. What should I do?

A

The serious disease tulip fire (*Botrytis tulipae*) has attacked your bulbs. It spreads very rapidly and infected bulbs should be dug up immediately and burned. The remaining bulbs should be sprayed thoroughly with a fungicide based on thiram or benomyl.

ROSE DISEASES

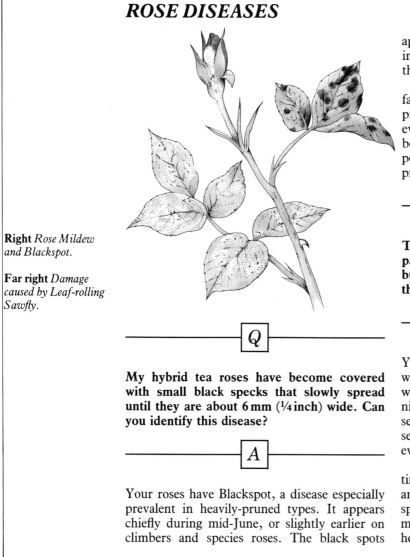

Right *Rose Mildew and Blackspot.*

Far right *Damage caused by Leaf-rolling Sawfly.*

appear on the lower leaves first, in time spreading higher up the plant. The spots join together, the leaf turns yellow and falls prematurely.

Blackspot can be controlled by burning all fallen leaves at the end of the season, and by picking off infected leaves. Spray the plants every two weeks with a fungicide based on benomyl, bupirimate/triforine, copper compound or dithane 945 after you have finished pruning the bushes in spring.

Q

The leaves on my roses have white powdery patches on them, and the bases of the flower buds are similarly covered. What is wrong with them and is there anything I can do?

A

Your roses have been attacked by Rose Mildew which is worst in wet summers and when the weather is warm during the day and cold at night. During dry, warm summers the disease is seldom seen. If left uncontrolled this disease will seriously mar the appearance of the plant and eventually kill the young buds.

Thinning out congested growths at pruning time will help to increase the circulation of air around the shoots. Also, using a proprietary spray, such as those based on benomyl, bupirimate and triforine or thiophanate methyl will help keep mildew in check.

Q

My hybrid tea roses have become covered with small black specks that slowly spread until they are about 6 mm (¼ inch) wide. Can you identify this disease?

A

Your roses have Blackspot, a disease especially prevalent in heavily-pruned types. It appears chiefly during mid-June, or slightly earlier on climbers and species roses. The black spots

Q

The blooms on my late-flowering outdoor chrysanthemums are turning brown and a greyish, velvety substance is rotting the leaves. What is troubling them?

A

Botrytis cinerea, commonly called Grey Mould. Encouraged by cool, damp conditions it attacks soft tissues on a range of plants from chrysanthemums and other herbaceous plants to bulbs, alpines, annuals, soft fruits and vegetables.

It is best to remove and burn all infected material. Ornamental plants can be dusted or sprayed with fungicides containing captan, thiram or zineb.

Above *The Honey Fungus* (Armillaria mellea) *often grows on dead tree stumps, but can spread to living roots with serious results.*

Q

My roses have leaves that are rolled, forming a tapering cylinder. What is the problem?

A

Your roses have been attacked by the Leaf-rolling Sawfly. If it is the first year your roses have been attacked pick off the affected leaves and burn them. If it has happened before, spray the plants with trichlorphon or fenitrothion in late April and again in early May.

Q

An old tree stump in my garden is covered with honey-coloured toadstools. Should I destroy them or are they harmless?

A

The toadstools are the result of a disease known as Honey Fungus. The actual toadstools do no harm, but the fungus itself overwinters in dead wood and then goes back into the soil where it will infect many subjects including herbaceous plants, roses, rhododendrons, some shrubs, bulbs and vegetables. Remove and destroy all affected plants, and drench the surrounding soil with a 2% solution of formalin.

The lawn is the other area in the garden that tends to be infested with toadstools. These are the well-known fairy rings, which appear as rings of toadstools on the grass. They have no visible effect on the grass and can be easily swept or mown off.

PESTS & DISEASES

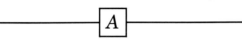

The leaves of my chrysanthemums are revealing black areas between the veins, and some of the lower leaves have turned completely black and shrivelled. Have you any idea what is causing the trouble?

The problem is caused by chrysanthemum leaf and bud eelworm, a pest that is most persistent and lives in dead tissue for many months. This microscopic worm-like creature penetrates the stems and leaves of chrysanthemums and also attacks many other ornamental plants. Its eradication is difficult and infected plants are best dug up and burned.

Infested plants should not be used for propagation. On a home gardener level there is, unfortunately, little one can do to control this pest, other than buying in healthy plants and growing them on a clean, fresh site. Whenever buying new plants make sure they are clean and not infected. Specialist growers use chemicals not available to home gardeners, as well as special propagation techniques that create healthy stock from which cuttings can be taken.

The flowers on both my dahlias and chrysanthemums are being chewed, but I have never seen any pest on the flowers. What can it be?

The flowers of these two highly decorative garden plants are prone to attack from earwigs. They feed mainly during warm evenings and nights, and will chew the leaves as well as the flowers. A general insecticide based on pyrethrum or pirimiphos-methyl, applied every fortnight, will control them.

Alternatively, to trap the pests, half-fill a pot with straw and invert over a cane or support among the flowers. Each morning shake the sheltering earwigs out of the pots into a bucket of boiling water to kill them.

The edges of my rhododendron leaves are being eaten away. What kind of pest is causing this damage?

The culprits are vine weevils, which chew the lower leaves, which are left looking tattered. They also eat the stems of ornamental shrubs. These weevils are small beetles with pronounced snouts. Spray at fortnightly intervals with a general insecticide such as pirimiphosmethyl or pyrethrum.

Some of my herbaceous plants are covered with frothy-like spit around the leaf joints. What is causing this?

This frothy substance – known as Cuckoo Spit – is created by the young forms of the common froghopper to protect them from birds. The adult attacks a wide range of plants, including roses, geum, solidago and lavender, and causes stems to wilt and to become distorted. The pest

Above *Rhododendron leaves damaged by Vine Weevils.*

Above right *A Common Green Capsid Bug, an agile, bright green insect, not easy to spot among foliage.*

Right *Cuckoo Spit, froth created by Common Froghoppers. Plants can be considerably weakened by their feeding activities.*

GREENFLY

Q

Many of my chrysanthemums, dahlias and roses are covered with a mass of small, greenish insects which cluster around soft shoot tips and buds. What are they?

A

They are most certain to be Greenfly, often called aphids. They attack the soft tissue, causing a weakening of the plants in general and distortion of all sucked tissue. They also transmit virus diseases that cause further problems. Use general aphid sprays based on pirimicarb, pirimiphos-methyl, or pyrethrum every ten days so that any insects that hatch since a previous treatment are killed. Sprays based on the insecticide pirimicarb will kill the aphids, but will not harm beneficial insects such as ladybirds, lacewings and hoverflies that feed on the aphids.

also transmits virus diseases. Spray with an insecticide such as permethrin, dimethoate or pirimicarb as soon as the pest is noticed. If the trouble persists, spray again after ten days.

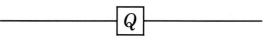

Q

My dahlias' young leaves are mottled and puckered with light, irregular spots.

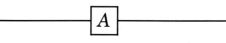

A

The insects causing this are the extremely active Common Green Capsid Bugs. They attack a wide range of plants, from chrysanthemums and dahlias to apples and currants. One aid to controlling these pests is to destroy all rubbish and weeds on which they can overwinter. Spray affected plants regularly throughout the summer with insecticides containing fenitrothion or gamma-HCH. Unfortunately, however, the pest has often departed from the plant before the damage becomes apparent.

Because of their soft-textured stems, leaves and flowers, dahlias are prone to attack from many pests and diseases. Leaf Spot or Smut produces circular brown spots on the lower leaves of bedding dahlias, which eventually turn black and shrivelling. Even the soft shoots at ground level can be attacked by Leafy Gall, becoming a mass of lumpy and distorted shoots. Infected plants are best dug up and burned.

SAFETY PRECAUTIONS

1. Read the instructions on the container and follow them to the letter. Do not add one for the pot.
2. Always wear rubber gloves when handling undiluted chemicals. Wash your hands and face afterwards.
3. Spray at the time indicated on the container, and also at the recommended intervals.
4. Spray in the evening or on dull days when bees and pollinating insects are not active.
5. Mix only as much spray as you can use. Flush surplus amounts of spray down the lavatory and dispose of empty containers by capping them tightly, wrapping them in a polythene bag and placing them in the dustbin.
6. Always use hand sprayers which are kept specifically for insecticide and fungicide application.
7. Do not spray garden chemicals on windy days or in bright sunshine, and do not spray into open flowers.
8. Store all chemicals in their original containers in a secure cupboard out of the reach of children and pets.
9. When spraying edible crops, always allow the recommended interval to elapse before harvesting.
10. Always wash all fruits and vegetables thoroughly before eating to remove all possible traces of chemicals.

VEGETABLES
PLANNING A KITCHEN GARDEN

I have soil-tested my new allotment and find that it has a pH of 6·5–7·5. What crops will grow best in it?

A

It is slightly on the alkaline (limy) side so parsnips and legumes including runner beans, broad beans and French beans will excel. So, too, will members of the cabbage family, which includes swedes and turnips. Carrots and lettuce grow well, too. But you may find that your soil's chalk content 'locks up' essential iron needed to produce the green colouring matter in the leaf, and in some instances leaves may be chlorotic, that is, yellowish with bright green veins. Overcome this problem by feeding with Sequestrene and adding bulky organic manure in autumn. Feed also with an acid-based nitrogenous fertilizer such as sulphate of ammonia.

Potatoes and rhubarb dislike limy conditions. If you would like to grow them, manure liberally and avoid using alkaline-based fertilizers.

Several years ago it was customary for many gardeners to scatter lime liberally over their soil every year, irrespective of the acidity or alkalinity of their soil. Nowadays, with the help of an inexpensive soil-testing kit, the correct amount of lime can be applied – if it is needed.

Q

My cabbages are growing lushly, with huge leaves, and are riddled with pests and diseases. How can I overcome this?

A

It is probable that your crop is suffering from too much nitrogen fertilizer which promotes soft growth vulnerable to attack by all kinds of garden troubles. For good growth, phosphate and potash also need to be present in balanced proportions. Carry out a soil test and apply a balanced compound fertilizer to ensure good growth in future crops.

CROP ROTATION

Q

What is crop rotation?

A

This is the rotation of certain types of vegetables on a piece of land, so that the same crops are not grown continuously in one position. Certain vegetables need different soil preparation and fertilizer and manure treatments from other vegetables. Also, growing a particular crop on the same piece of land year after year encourages the build up of soil pests and diseases.

Plants can be grouped in three broad types – *seed and stem crops* (group A), *root crops* (group B) and *greens* (group C). The vegetable plot can be divided into three equal parts and within each part over a three-year period a different type of vegetable can be grown.

	PLOT 1	PLOT 2	PLOT 3
YEAR 1	A	B	C
YEAR 2	B	C	A
YEAR 3	C	A	B

GROUP A	GROUP B	GROUP C
Bean crops	Beetroot	Broccoli
Cucumbers	Carrots	Brussels
Celery	Parsnips	sprouts
Leeks	Potatoes	Cabbages
Lettuce	Swedes	Cauliflowers
Marrows		Turnips
Onions		
Peas		
Shallots		
Spinach		
Sweetcorn		

GROWING BAGS

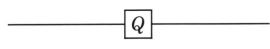

I only have a patio on which to grow plants. Is it possible to grow vegetables in growing bags?

───── A ─────

Yes indeed. Growing bags are ideal for raising a range of vegetables on your patio. Do not try to grow deep-rooted vegetables, such as parsnips and swedes in growing bags. Rather, concentrate on salad crops such as lettuces, spring onions, cucumbers and tomatoes. You might also like to try dwarf beans.

───── Q ─────

What do the initials N P K mean?

───── A ─────

These stand for the major foods required by plants. N means *nitrogen*, P stands for *phosphate* and K for *potassium*, better known as potash. For strong growth, it is essential that these chemicals are present in the correct amounts to suit the particular crop and its stage of development. For instance, during their early stages tomato plants require more nitrogen than the other major foods so that they can develop plenty of leaves and shoots. But later, when the fruits are ripening, more potash is needed.

───── Q ─────

I've heard that mulching benefits growth. What is a mulch and how do I use it?

───── A ─────

A mulch can be organic – old manure, well rotted garden compost, grass cuttings, straw, peat or pulverized bark – or plastic. Its purpose is to conserve soil moisture in droughty spells in summer, keep down weeds and warm the soil to encourage early growth. Organic mulches also feed plants and are usually much more pleasant to look at than plastic types, and are, therefore, preferred by many gardeners.

However, if you choose to use a plastic mulch, use black plastic as it excludes light, thereby keeping down weeds, and absorbs sun heat to keep soil warm but moist, and speeds rapid growth. Unroll the black plastic between the rows and, to anchor it, sprinkle earth over the edges where they butt up to the plants.

When using black plastic mulches, scatter slug bait liberally before positioning the plastic, as the dark, warmth and moisture create an ideal environment for the creatures.

When mulching roses with organic material such as crumbly, decayed manure, in early spring, wait until the soil is free from frost and warmed by the sun.

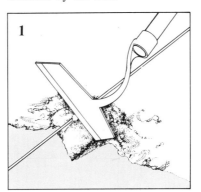

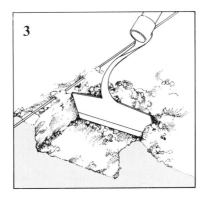

MAKING SEED DRILLS
Several different types of seed drills are used, depending on the seeds to be sown in them. For instance, a V-drill (1) formed with the edge of a draw hoe is ideal for small seeds. A narrow flat-bottomed drill (2) is suitable for potatoes and a wide-bottomed drill (3) is ideal for seeds such as peas.

SPECIFIC VEGETABLES

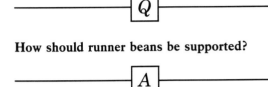

How should runner beans be supported?

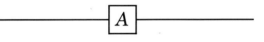

Several methods can be used. Traditionally, bean poles are used but these are often difficult to obtain. Strong netting stretched between two stout posts is a useful method if you wish to grow the beans across the width of your plot. Alternatively, a wig-wam formed of canes or a may-pole arrangement of strings are useful when positioning the beans in small plots or awkward-shaped corners.

Try to position your runner beans within range of a hose pipe, as these vegetables need plenty of water.

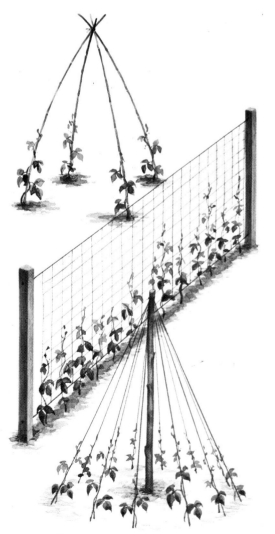

3 methods of supporting runner beans:
Top *A cane wig-wam.*
Middle *Netting stretched between two posts.*
Bottom *A maypole arrangement of strings.*

I saw a lettuce in a greengrocer shop which had many small leaves, and did not form a heart like most types. What is it and when should I sow seeds?

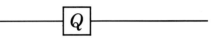

It is a leaf type, and most probably the variety 'Salad Bowl', which produces a mass of small leaves within fifty days of being sown. From April to mid-May sow seeds thinly and 12 mm (½ inch) deep in drills spaced 130–150 mm (5–6 inches) apart.

Being somewhat ornamental it can be used to edge a flower border. Leaves are gathered regularly and many more sprout to replace them.

I would like to grow asparagus. What is the best method?

The first step is to choose a high-yielding variety such as 'Lorella', which has thick, milky, green-tipped stems.

Select a patch of well-manured soil and top-dress with 50 g (2 oz) per sq. yd. of bonemeal and the same of superphosphate plus 25 g (1 oz) per sq. yd. of sulphate of potash.

Set the roots, which are long and spidery, on a rounded ridge of soil in a trench so the crowns (top, budded portion) are 100 mm (4 inches) below the surface. Space crowns 300 mm (1 ft) apart in three rows 300 mm (1 ft) apart. Then divide the three-row section with a 750 mm (2½ ft) path.

To help plants become well established, do not cut any spears in the first season after planting. In subsequent seasons, start cutting when spears are 150 mm (6 inches) above the soil. Cease harvesting in late June to allow ferny leaves to develop and strengthen growth for the next year.

Feed with 100 g (4 oz) dressing of balanced fertilizer each spring and follow with a thick mulch of old manure or well rotted garden compost.

In autumn, the ferny leaves turn brown and should be cut back to soil level.

POLLINATING MARROWS

Q

Is it necessary to hand-pollinate marrows?

A

Pollination usually takes place on its own with help from visiting insects, but during cold weather, or early in the year, hand-pollination may be necessary. The female flowers – those appearing to be sitting on small marrows – need to have a male flower, when it is releasing pollen, dusted over them.

During prolonged cold weather it may be necessary to repeat this hand-pollinating several times, until the weather improves and the insects return.

Q

How many bunches should I allow to form on my outdoor tomatoes before nipping out their tops and stopping them?

A

Allow four bunches, or trusses, to develop. As soon as the fruits on the fourth truss are swelling, either cut off or bend and snap the leading shoot, two leaves above the top truss.

Q

Is it necessary to cut off the tops of leeks before they are planted?

A

Yes, as it helps the newly-planted seedlings to become established quickly. Also, trim off about one-third of the roots to ensure that the young plant rests on the bottom of the hole which should be 230–300 mm (9–12 inches) deep. A thorough watering at that stage settles the plant in the hole. Do not pack the holes with soil as the plants need room to swell.

If the soil becomes dry during subsequent weeks, water the plants. This will eventually return soil to the hole and help to settle it around the roots.

Q

In previous years I've noticed birds tugging at my onion sets. Many are completely displaced. How can I prevent this?

A

Simple – cut off the wispy tops which protrude through the soil, attracting the birds. Use sharp scissors to snip off the tops, then set them with their tips slightly above the surface. Use a trowel to plant them 100–150 mm (4–6 inches) apart in rows 300 mm (1 ft) apart.

To discourage birds, it may be necessary to cover onions initially with wire-netting formed into tunnels. As soon as the onion sets have become well rooted the wire can be removed. Incidentally, frost can also lift the soil and make the sets loose. If this happens replant them immediately, firming the soil around them.

Below left When planting leeks, do not firm the soil, but water in so the growing plant can swell more easily.

Below right Snip off the top of onion sets to prevent birds pulling at them when nest-building.

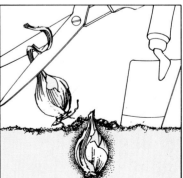

SPECIFIC VEGETABLES

I would like to grow an early crop of potatoes and would appreciate your advice.

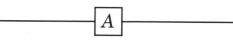

Start with a 'first early' variety such as 'Dunluce', 'Foremost' or 'Maris Bard'. Sprout the tubers by setting them eye-end uppermost in seed trays or egg cartons, in a light, warm place. (The temperature should not be over 13–16°C (55–60°F) or the shoots will grow spindly.)

When the soil is fit to cultivate in March or early April take out drills 150 mm (6 inches) deep and 600 mm (2 ft) apart and space the tubers 375 mm (15 inches) apart with their shoots uppermost. If the soil is poor, sprinkle a thin layer of processed manure along the bottom of the drill before setting tubers in position. Cover with soil.

When shoots push through the soil, earth up the rows, i.e. use a swan-necked hoe to ridge the soil up round the plants, to protect the frost-tender leaves. Another earthing-up when a further 150 mm (6 inches) of growth is made will ensure that developing tubers remain below the soil and stay blanched and edible.

Scatter fertilizer at 100 g (4 oz) per sq.yd. along the rows to speed development when the leaves are 300 mm (1 ft) or so above the soil in mid-June. Water freely in dry weather.

Another method of growing early potatoes is to plant two or three seed potatoes that already have sprouts (small shoots) growing from them in a large pot or box. Cover them with cloches (see pages 46–47), with extra protection from sacking whenever frost threatens.

ONIONS AND LEEKS

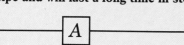

How are large onions harvested to ensure they are fully ripe and will last a long time in store?

During late August or early September, bend the tops so that the rows are bent alternately to the left and right, so that you can walk between the rows. Use a fork to break the roots, still leaving the bulbs in rows to assist ripening. Make sure the base plate (bottom of the bulb) faces upwards to be ripened by the sun. Ideally, cover bulbs if rain threatens, to prevent them splitting and growing out from the base.

Is there any special way to lift leeks from the soil? I don't want to damage them.

Use a strong garden fork, taking care not to damage the blanched stems. Although a hand can be placed on the stem, do not pull the plant up by this as it can quickly be damaged.

Using a strong garden fork, insert this well down beside the leek stem. Then, gently holding the green shaft, taking care not to wrench at it, for it will break, lever up on the fork and prise out the plant.

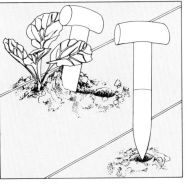

Q

Is it essential to use a dibber to plant cabbages and other brassicas?

A

No, using a trowel is an alternative method, but a dibber does enable each plant to be set firmly in the soil. Push the dibber well into the soil, place the young plant in position – with the part where the leaves join the stem just above soil-level – and then use the dibber to lever soil against the roots. A test to ensure it is planted firmly is to try to pull off a leaf. If the leaf breaks then the plant has been set firmly in the soil.

Q

My neighbour always nips out the tips of his broad bean plants. Is this essential?

A

It looks a destructive practice, but it has two vital effects on the plants. Firstly, it reduces the danger from Black Bean Aphids that enjoy sucking sap from the soft tips. Secondly, it encourages a more uniform development of pods on the plant. It is best done when the plants are in full flower, removing the top 100–150 mm (4–6 inches) of each shoot, when on each stem 4 clusters, or trusses, of pods have formed.

If the tips are already infested with Black Bean Aphids, they are best put in an incinerator immediately. To prevent the aphids escaping, first put the tips in a plastic bag.

Q

Is it essential to grow celery in trenches?

A

Many years ago this was essential, but now there are several superb so-called 'self-blanching' varieties that can be grown on the flat. The plants are set close together, so that each excludes light from its neighbour. (Growing celery in full light will result in stringy, less succulent growth.) Pieces of boarding around the outside will prevent light reaching plants at the perimeter. Suitable varieties include 'Lathom Self-Blanching' and 'Golden Self-Blanching'.

Q

Friends tell me I should grow my sweetcorn in blocks rather than rows. Why is this?

A

Because sweetcorn is pollinated by wind it is essential that the plants are set in blocks of plants rather than long single rows. Then the chance is very much greater of the female, tassel-like flowers receiving pollen.

Q

I am keen to grow exhibition parsnips. Can you give me any tips?

A

Get the best roots by using a crowbar to form holes up to 900 mm (3 ft) deep and 380 mm (15 inches) apart. Fill with sifted soil or old potting compost laced with a balanced fertilizer mixture. Choose a sunny site.

'Tender and True' and 'Cobham Improved Marrow' are excellent exhibition varieties, having long tapering roots.

In March, or as soon as the soil is warming nicely, sow three seeds per hole, thinning to the strongest when three or four leaves have formed.

Water freely in dry spells, keep weeded and top-dress with a high-potash fertilizer in mid-May and mid-July. Stop the top of the root, where it joins the leaf stalks, from splitting by covering with a thick layer of peat.

Guard against Celery Fly, which also attacks parsnips, by spraying with a permethrin-based insecticide in early June and repeat two or three times at 10 day intervals.

Lift the roots carefully, excavating soil from around them so as not to break the much prized taper acclaimed by the judges.

Above left *Use a dibber to plant cabbages, levering the dibber to firm the soil against the roots.*

Above right *Test cabbage to see that it is firmly planted – a small portion of the leaf should tear away without shifting the plant.*

THE HERB GARDEN

Q

What is the best aspect for a herb garden?

A

Preferably, choose a border relatively close to your house, which is sunny, well-drained and facing south. Light shade for part of the day is acceptable to many herbs. Interestingly, a poor soil, which is somewhat short of nutrients, promotes stronger flavour and scents.

Q

Last year my parsley failed to germinate. Have you any idea what I may have done wrong?

A

Parsley is difficult to germinate if the soil dries out. In fact, in extremely dry years it may not germinate at all. During this coming year, sow seeds in drills that have had a drop of water trickled into their bases. After sowing, cover the seeds with dry soil. This will help to retain moisture around the seeds.

Below *Borage is an attractive plant which is easy to grow.*

Q

Is it possible to grow a bay tree in a container, as I only have a small terraced garden?

A

Bay trees grow particularly well in large tubs, and are especially eye-catching when a pair of them are positioned either side of a doorway. Painting the container white makes the effect even more stunning. Protect them from cold winds which often damage the leaves.

If you live in an area with a high winter rainfall, it may be necessary to cover the soil in the pot with a piece of polythene or two tiles. The easiest method involves using the polythene, tying it around the pot with strong string or wire. If the compost in the pot is allowed to become saturated, there is a chance that the entire root ball will freeze, causing damage to the roots.

Q

What herbs can I grow from seeds each year?

A

There are many superb sorts that can be raised from seeds each year, such as:

Basil (*Ocimum basilicum*). A half-hardy annual, growing 600–900 mm (2–3 ft) high with fleshy stems and thick leaves 75 mm (3 inches) long, and with a strong smell of cloves. Delicious in cooked tomato dishes.

Borage (*Borago officinalis*). An annual, rising 450–600 mm (1½–2 ft) high. It is a plant with bristly and hairy leaves and beautiful, bright blue, star-like flowers borne in clusters. Chopped leaves flavour salads and wine cups.

Sweet Marjoram (*Origanum majorana*). A perennial usually treated as an annual. It grows 200–250 mm (8–10 inches) high (more when grown as a perennial), with grey-green leaves and white flowers in July. Use to enrich meat, fish and tomato dishes. Good in salads, too.

Parsley (*Pelroselinum crispum*). A biennial, often treated as an annual, and growing 150–200 mm (6–8 inches) high. Its curled and deeply-divided leaves are well known. Garnish for fish and meat dishes. Nourishing when used in soups and stews.

Above *The herb garden can be a delightful feature as well as a useful and productive part of the garden. Many herbs have attractive flowers or foliage, and there is usually the bonus of fragrance.*

Q

Can any herbs be picked fresh in winter?

A

There are several to choose from, such as Chervil (*Anthriscus cerefolium*) which is sown during August and September and will withstand most winters outside. As a substitute for chives you could grow either Welsh onions or perennial onions. Raise the Welsh onions from seed or by dividing old lumps in spring or autumn. It is possible to use both the leaves and the bulbs. Perennial onions, which look like pale chives, must be raised by division. Parsley can be sown during July for a winter supply, but it tends to be cut back by cold weather unless protected with cloches (see pages 46–47).

Other evergreen herbs are Thyme, Rosemary, Pot Marjoram and Winter Savory. These, as well as chervil, fare better if given the protection of frames or cloches during winter.

Q

I have a small round border previously used for roses. Can I convert this successfully into a herb garden? And which plants do you suggest I grow?

A

A small round bed of herbs can look very attractive and provide a wide range of culinary herbs. You will need to section off the bed; small pebbles or narrow edging blocks can be used for this purpose.

Invasive plants, such as mint, are best left in their pots; bury them so that the rims are 50 mm (2 inches) above the soil's surface.

To prevent the herbs spilling over into another section, trim them each year.

In the plot above, clockwise from the top are: a bay tree, rosemary, tarragon, chives, chervil, sage, thyme (lemon and common), parsley, marjoram, angelica, applemint and spearmint.

GREENHOUSES

Where in my garden should I position my greenhouse, and what is the best shape for it?

If you have a choice, the best option is a bright, open site which is not shaded by trees that stop sunlight and drip water over the greenhouse long after a storm has passed. Rectangular greenhouses are usually the best shape, with the ridge running east to west to allow the maximum amount of winter sunlight to reach the plants.

Do I need to have a water-butt by the side of my greenhouse, to water my plants?

Below *A lean-to greenhouse with roof and side ventilators. Narrow-section glazing bars cut out the minimum of light.*

Most water-butts become a haven for all sorts of pests and diseases. It is better to use water straight from a mains tap. However, you can sterilize the water by adding a few crystals of potassium permanganate – just enough to turn the water light pink.

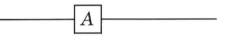

I will not be able to heat my greenhouse. Is it still worth having one?

Very much so. Even without the benefit of artificial heating, a greenhouse is still useful for a whole range of plants that need only weather protection and are semi-hardy as far as temperature is concerned. And even without heat, by April the warmth from the sun will be sufficient for early sowings of many seeds and the propagation of some plants such as French marigolds (*tagetes*) and dahlias.

I have some heating in my greenhouse, but do not allow the temperature to go above 7°C (45°F) or below freezing. Which greenhouse plants would suit this temperature?

There is a wide range you can choose from, including many fuchsias, pelargoniums, cineraria, primulas, calceolarias, and tender bulbs. Many annuals such as tagetes, zinnias and pansies can also be raised at these temperatures, and there is a wide range of greenhouse shrubs, such as yellow-flowered acacias and *Albizia julibrissin*, which is prized for its head of bright pink flowers.

Is it better to have a lean-to greenhouse, rather than a free-standing one?

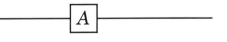

A greenhouse with connecting doors such as French windows to the house is ideal. The house helps to keep the greenhouse warm, and the greenhouse, if on a south-facing wall, will add warmth to the house and will also help to eliminate draughts. As lean-to greenhouses are more accessible than free-standing types, they are often made more use of.

Q

My greenhouse has no staging in it. Can I grow crops directly into the border soil?

A

It is best not to do this, especially for edible crops like tomatoes and cucumbers. If these are grown repeatedly in the same patch of soil the ground becomes 'sick' and further crops are unsuccessful. If, too, the soil becomes a reservoir of pests and diseases from infected crops it is very difficult to eradicate them. Grow your crops in pots or other containers, including growing-bags, to avoid these problems.

Right Tomatoes in growing bags.

GREENHOUSE HEATING

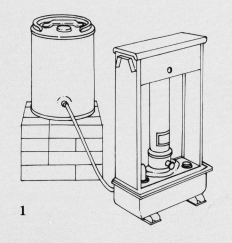

1

2

3

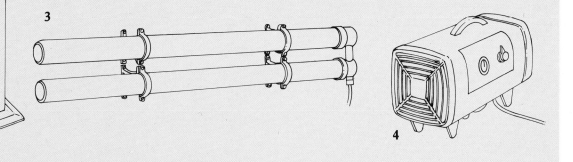

4

Q

I have a small greenhouse which I want to heat only in early spring. What is the best method?

A

A small paraffin heater would be the easiest method. But it may be necessary to ask a member of your family or a neighbour to turn off the heating during early spring mornings when the frost is late to clear and you have left for work. Check the heater every week to ensure the paraffin is burning cleanly – there should be an even blue flame – and trim the wick regularly. Make sure you leave a chink of air at all times except in frosty weather.

There is a wide choice of greenhouse heaters. Some use solid fuels; others use gas, oil or electricity. Whatever the heat source, costs increase steeply with quite modest increments of temperature. It costs twice as much to heat to 13°C (55°F) as it does to heat to 7°C (45°F), and three times as much to heat to 16°C (60°F).

1 *Paraffin-oil heaters are economical if used just to keep out frost or maintain cool greenhouse conditions.*

2 *Thermostatically-controlled natural or propane gas heaters are efficient and require little maintenance.*

3 *Electric (black-heat) tubular heaters are economical to use, especially if thermostatically controlled. No maintenance needed.*

4 *Electric fan heaters, if coupled to a thermostat, provide the most convenient and versatile means of warming the greenhouse. Heating is almost instantaneous and of a buoyant nature. Only an annual overhaul required.*

FRAMES & CLOCHES

COLD FRAMES

Q

I have an old-fashioned wooden-sided garden frame in my new garden. Can you please tell me what I can use it for?

A

During spring you will find the frame useful for raising early crops of lettuce, radish, or carrots. Also, you could raise seedlings in it.

In summer the frame is ideal for growing melons or cucumbers, which can be trained horizontally. Because of the limited amount of light this type of frame admits, it is not suitable for winter crops, but it can be used for over-wintering seedlings of summer cauliflowers, lettuces, and autumn-sown varieties of onions. In addition, it can be used for forcing chicory or blanching endives.

Frames are available in a wide variety of styles and sizes. The traditional wooden-box type is generally the cheapest and remains as useful as any. Some versions have asbestos sides. The modern glass-sided design with a span roof is useful for light-demanding winter crops such as lettuce.

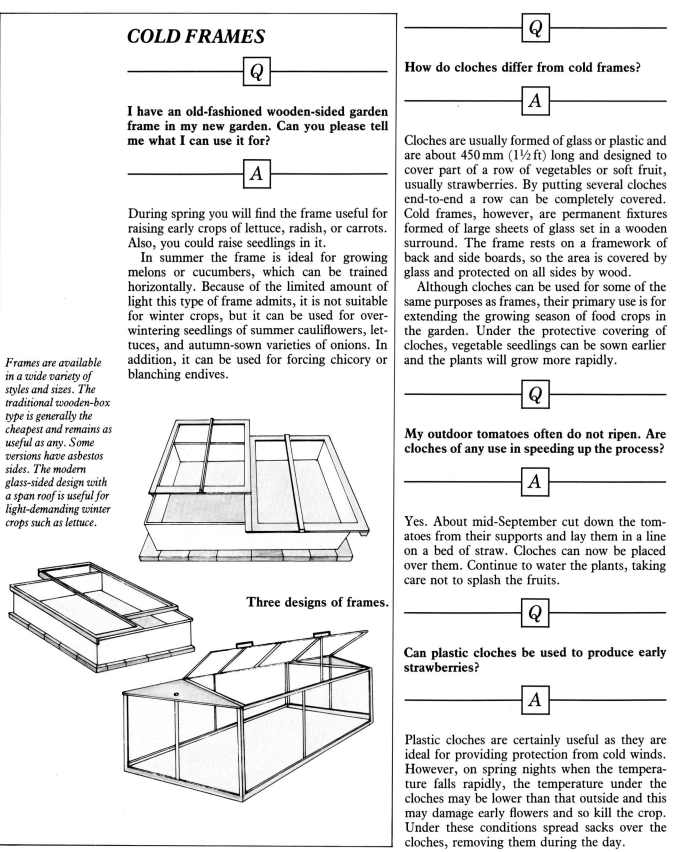

Three designs of frames.

Q

How do cloches differ from cold frames?

A

Cloches are usually formed of glass or plastic and are about 450 mm (1½ ft) long and designed to cover part of a row of vegetables or soft fruit, usually strawberries. By putting several cloches end-to-end a row can be completely covered. Cold frames, however, are permanent fixtures formed of large sheets of glass set in a wooden surround. The frame rests on a framework of back and side boards, so the area is covered by glass and protected on all sides by wood.

Although cloches can be used for some of the same purposes as frames, their primary use is for extending the growing season of food crops in the garden. Under the protective covering of cloches, vegetable seedlings can be sown earlier and the plants will grow more rapidly.

Q

My outdoor tomatoes often do not ripen. Are cloches of any use in speeding up the process?

A

Yes. About mid-September cut down the tomatoes from their supports and lay them in a line on a bed of straw. Cloches can now be placed over them. Continue to water the plants, taking care not to splash the fruits.

Q

Can plastic cloches be used to produce early strawberries?

A

Plastic cloches are certainly useful as they are ideal for providing protection from cold winds. However, on spring nights when the temperature falls rapidly, the temperature under the cloches may be lower than that outside and this may damage early flowers and so kill the crop. Under these conditions spread sacks over the cloches, removing them during the day.

FRENCH BEANS

Q

How can I use cloches to produce early crops of dwarf French beans?

A

During early spring prepare a strip of soil for planting and place cloches over it to warm up the earth. In early April sow seeds under the cloches. The crop will be ready during late June. Remember, that for successful and quick germination of bean seeds the soil needs to be at least 10°C (50°F). Cold and wet soils encourage the seeds to rot. In cold areas wait until late April or early May before sowing seeds. Always choose a sunny but sheltered position.

Q

Are plastic cloches better than glass ones?

A

Glass transmits light more easily than plastic, and conserves heat better, especially at night. However, plastic is more durable and does not break so easily as glass. If you have inquisitive or energetic children it might be better to use plastic. However, plastic cloches are more likely to be blown away during fierce winds. If you do buy plastic types, ensure they have been treated with ultra-violet inhibitors as they last longer.

Q

What are polythene tunnels and what are their advantages?

A

Polythene tunnels are formed of polythene sheeting stretched over wire hoops to form a tunnel. Further wire hoops are used to prevent the plastic sheeting blowing away. Polythene tunnels are used widely in commercial horticulture. They are far cheaper than greenhouses, need no foundations and are quickly erected. They can also be moved from one place to another quite easily. The polythene transmits light and retains heat, enabling the tunnels to be used in the same way as cloches, The crops are ventilated either by leaving the ends of the tunnel open or by rolling up the polythene from one of the sides.

However, one of the disadvantages of polythene tunnels is that they are not very durable. The polythene can easily be torn and then has to be replaced.

Left *The traditional glass barn cloche, ideal for advancing early crops.*

Above *Corrugated rigid plastic tunnel cloches are easier to handle than polythene and longer-lasting, but much more expensive initially.*

PESTS & DISEASES

Above *Blackfly on a broad bean plant.*

Above right *A Cutworm.*

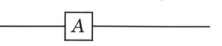

Many of my lettuce seedlings are toppling over, and have the appearance of being chewed at the base. What is affecting them?

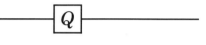

It is probably Cutworms. These are dull-green, caterpillar-like pests that chew stems at or about ground level, causing the seedlings to fall over. Dust soil around the seedlings with gamma-HCH or bromophos.

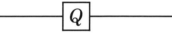

My broad beans are covered by small black flies. What should I do?

These are a form of aphids, variously known as Blackfly, Black Dolphin, Blight or Black Army. Whatever the name, they are very destructive and are usually seen at the end of May or early June. As well as attacking broad beans, they attack spinach, turnips, parsnips, rhubarb and dahlias. On broad beans they cluster around the soft shoot tips, and may then spread to pods and leaves. Nip out the tips of shoots and spray with a derris or permethrin insecticide.

Are centipedes as harmful to vegetables as millipedes?

No, they are beneficial. Centipedes have only one pair of legs on each body segment and are therefore able to run faster than the sluggish millipede that has two pairs of legs on each body segment. Centipedes feed on soil creatures, some of which are plant pests, and are able to chase prey that moves, while millipedes have to restrict themselves to plants.

CABBAGE DISEASES

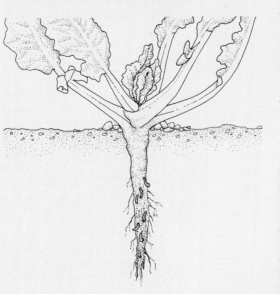

Many of my cabbage plants are wilting and taking on a bluish appearance. What could be the trouble?

It seems likely that the plants have been attacked by Cabbage Root Fly (*Delia brassicae*). Dig up one end of the infected plants and examine the roots and base of the stem for the presence of maggots.

Early attacks by this pest can be prevented by dusting a soil insecticide on to the seed drills and the transplanted plants. Later attacks can be dealt with by applying a heavy soil drench of spray-strength pirimiphos-methyl or trichlorphon.

VEGETABLE PESTS AND THEIR CONTROL

PEST	CROPS AFFECTED	DESCRIPTION	CONTROL
Carrot Fly Maggot (*Psila rosae*)	Carrots, celery, parsley and parsnips	Small white maggots in roots. Leaves of affected plants often turn bronze	Bromophos
Caterpillars (*Lepidoptera*)	Brassica crops	Well-known to all gardeners. Many different kinds, most belonging to moths	Carbaryl, rotenone and quassia
Cockchafer (*Melolontha melolontha*)	Soft fruit, potatoes and herbaceous plants	Beetle, 2·5 cm (1 in) long, black head and thorax, reddish-brown wing cases. Eats leaves; grubs eat roots	Bromophos (for grubs)
Leatherjackets (*Tipula*)	Grasses, herbaceous plants and vegetables	The larvae of crane-flies. Resemble dark grey or black caterpillars, but have no legs	Gamma-HCH; methiocarb
Onion Fly Maggot (*Delia antiqua*)	Onions, leeks, shallots	Small white maggots attack onion bulbs at or just below soil level. Foliage droops	Bromophos; mercurous chloride
Turnip Flea Beetles (*Phyllotreta*)	Turnips, cabbages, broccoli, sprouts	Small black beetles that make small round holes in leaves, especially seedlings.	Gamma-HCH; rotenone; carbaryl
Whiteflies (*Aleyrodidae*)	Tomatoes in greenhouses, cabbage family outdoors	Tiny white flying insects, sometimes rising when disturbed, to form a white cloud	Bioresmethrin aerosol (for greenhouses); dimethoate (systemic); malathon

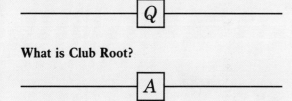

What is Club Root?

This is a disease that attacks all members of the cabbage family, including turnips and even ornamental plants of the cruciferae family such as wallflowers and stocks. The disease is also known as Finger-and-Toe or Anbury. It is a fungus disease that destroys the small roots and causes larger ones to become knotted, gnarled and swollen. The roots begin to smell and the whole plant is stunted. Leaves turn yellow and the plants wilt in hot weather. The disease is encouraged by wet, poorly-drained and acid soil. A way of controlling it is to improve drainage, add lime and to dig in plenty of bulky organic material, such as well-rotted garden compost, peat, pulverized bark, processed manures. Another step to take before setting any plants in the soil, is to dust the drills or planting holes with a proprietary clubroot powder containing thiophanate-methyl.

FRUIT

FRUIT TREES

I want to plant a plum that is suitable for dessert and culinary purposes.

You could not do better than 'Victoria'. It is self-fertile, so you do not need to plant other plum varieties close by. It produces heavy crops of large, oval, bright red fruits during late August. The plums are sometimes speckled with darker dots, and may have a golden-yellow flush.

Below *Plum 'Victoria', which has an excellent flavour.*

As I do not have anywhere to store apples, please suggest a variety I can eat as soon as it is picked.

The variety 'James Grieve', with a rich, juicy flavour, is superb straight from the tree. It is dependable and crops heavily, with oval or irregularly-shaped fruits which have a red flush over-laying a pale yellow colour. Its one draw-back is that it bruises easily – so take care when picking.

It does, however, need a pollinating partner to ensure regular crops. Choose from crisp and juicy, October to November ripening 'Jester', and orange-red-skinned 'Jupiter', a firm, juicy variety which is ready for picking from October to November.

For some years now my apple tree has made strong shoots and few flowers, hence few fruits. How can I encourage it to crop well and regularly again?

Curb excessive shoot growth and stimulate the development of fruit spurs – which bear flowers, then apples – by root pruning and bark ringing.

Root pruning is done in winter. Take out a trench around the tree some 900 mm (3 ft) from the trunk and cut through all roots. This will encourage fine, feeding roots to form and will slow down leaf growth. Anchor the tree against high winds by fixing three guy lines to it.

Bark ringing is carried out in May, when the tree is in flower. Make two cuts 5 mm (¼ inch) apart round the trunk and peel off the bark between them. Seal the wound with waterproof tape to exclude air and speed healing. In autumn, when the cut has callused over, remove the tape.

In a year or two this treatment will result in plenty of flowers and good crops most years.

What are the best rootstocks for apples, bearing in mind that I do not want a large tree?

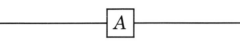

There are many rootstocks used for apples, but only dwarf or semi-dwarf ones are suitable for the amateur. The dwarf ones are Malling 27 (M27), giving a tree up to 1·2 m (4 ft) high, Malling No 9 (M IX), producing growth up to 2·4 m (8 ft) high, and Malling 26 (M26). Semi-dwarfing ones are M VII and MM106 which impart much stronger growth, up to 3·5–4·5 m (12–15 ft).

The wisdom of selecting a dwarf rootstock can often be seen when visiting old orchards, where many of the fruits are too high to be picked.

Please suggest several pear varieties which are ready at different times so that I can eat these fruits over a long period.

Pears are available for eating from September to January. Two September varieties are 'William's Bon Chrétien', a heavy and reliable cropper with juicy and sweet fruits, and 'Bristol Cross' which is ready in October as well as September and bears good flavoured juicy fruits; some people prefer it to 'Conference'. For November 'Doyenné du Comice' is superb, being the finest flavoured pear, while the well-known 'Winter Nelis' can be eaten right through from November to January.

TRAINING FRUIT TREES

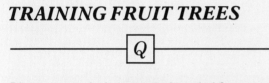

I have a west-facing closely-boarded fence and would like to grow fruit trees along it. What form of tree should I plant?

It is certainly possible to train fruit trees to grow along a fence or wall and there are many advantages in doing so, the greatest being that space is used economically, an important consideration in small gardens. The small size of trees grown in this way makes them easy to look after; the fruit can be picked effortlessly and pruning can be carried out without a ladder. The trees provide as much fruit as larger ones and in a much shorter time. There are various methods of training fruit trees.

Cordons are trained on a single stem tied to wires and are grown at an angle along a wall, fence or series of wires strained between posts.

An **espalier** is another form of tree with restricted growth. A central stem is trained vertically while tiers of horizontal branches are tied to wires. Building up the framework of an espalier takes time and skill, but the end result justifies the effort involved.

Cordons and espaliers are particularly suitable for growing apples. Peaches, nectarines and cherries can be trained in a fan-shape, with branches radiating out in the style of a fan.

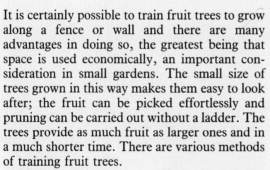

Left *Cordons trained at an oblique angle.*

Below *A mature fruiting espalier.*

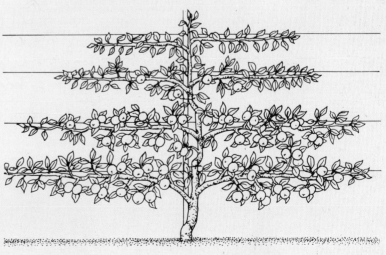

SOFT FRUIT

Q

How does the pruning of blackcurrants and redcurrants differ?

A

These fruits require totally different treatments; blackcurrants are grown as 'stooled' plants with the majority of new shoots arising from soil-level, whereas redcurrants are grown on a 'leg' with a permanent framework of shoots.

After blackcurrants have fruited and the crop has been picked, cut out all fruited wood to within 25 mm (1 inch) of soil-level.

It is essential that weak twigs and damaged or diseased wood are also cut out, together with any particularly low branches from which the black-currants may rub on the ground and become damaged.

With redcurrants, when the framework has been established, all that is needed is to cut back the growth produced that year to 25 mm (1 inch) of where it originated. The oldest dark wood can be cut back hard and new shoots from low down should be trained in to take its place.

Far right *Cordon-trained gooseberry bushes take up little space and are useful in small gardens.*

Below *Protect strawberry fruits by laying straw.*

Q

Please suggest several raspberry varieties that are suitable for freezing and for desserts.

A

There are several you could consider, such as 'Glen Clova' with medium to large fruits from July to August, 'Lloyd George' with large dark-ish red fruits during July, 'Malling Jewel' with bright red berries becoming darker as they open, during July and August, and 'Norfolk Giant' with heavy and regular crops of bright red, conical berries during August.

Q

Is there an alpine strawberry suitable for jam-making?

A

Yes. These runnerless alpine strawberries are long-cropping and ideal for dessert use as well as for making preserves. 'Baron Solemacher' and 'Alexandria' are ideal varieties, with fruits from June to October.

Q

Every year my strawberries are spoilt because heavy thunderstorms splash mud onto the fruits. Is there anything I can do to avoid this happening?

A

You can either spread straw between the rows and under the plants when the fruits are starting to form, or grow the plants in small holes cut in black polythene. Or buy special discs that are easily slipped round the crowns.

As well as heavy rain storms, birds can be a problem with strawberries – and, indeed, other fruits. For this reason it is worth considering covering the fruits with loose netting stretched over a low framework, or building a special wire-netting fruit cage. Many home gardeners do find it a permanent solution as birds can destroy buds as well as fruits.

I have a small garden and wish to grow gooseberries. Is this possible?

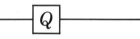

Yes, but you may have to grow them as cordons, trained up a series of wire supports. Plant them in a good sunny position sheltered from cold winds and late-spring frosts. When gooseberries are grown as cordons they require special pruning in midsummer. Remove all surplus shoots and shorten side shoots to five leaves from the old wood to form fruiting spurs.

Is there such a thing as a thornless loganberry? I am fed up with being scratched by thorns!

The variety 'LY 654,' which produces red berries, is well worth trying. It is excellent for cooking or bottling, with berries during July and August.

RASPBERRIES

Is it essential to have a series of wires up which raspberries can be trained?

Yes, as some means of support is necessary to prevent the canes from snapping in the wind and to make it easy to pick the fruit. The easiest method is to erect posts at each end of the rows, stretching two strands of wire between them, the lowest being about 450 mm (18 inches) above the ground, and the second being 1·5 m (5 ft) above the ground. If the canes are not very strong, use more wires and space them about 300 mm (12 inches) apart. These canes support the young canes that develop each year as well as the canes made the previous year.

Raspberry canes bear fruits during their second year. Once picking has finished, cut out all fruited canes, tying in the new canes to replace them. Allow four or five new canes to each stool, removing all others, particularly those which are weak or small. Always keep the crop well picked, as over-ripe fruit left on the canes is liable to attack from mildew and other fungus disorders.

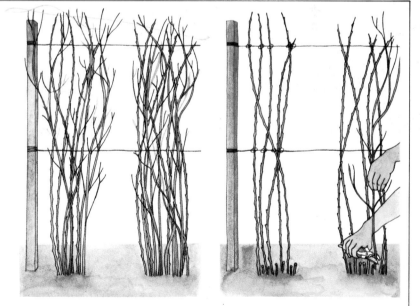

Above *Training and pruning raspberry canes.*

PESTS & DISEASES

Above *Peach Leaf Curl is a particularly disfiguring disease.*

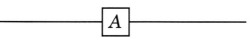

My peach tree has leaves that exhibit reddish blisters, becoming raised and swollen with a whitish bloom on some leaves. What can I do?

These are the symptoms of Peach Leaf Curl, a disease causing leaves to fall prematurely with the result that the tree is weakened. It is a serious problem and the tree must be sprayed with mancozeb or a copper-based fungicide at leaf fall and again in late January and early February. Also, all infected leaves must be collected and burned.

If left unchecked, this disease prevents the development and formation of fruit buds and the tree eventually becomes useless. The disease also attacks nectarines and almonds, although if grown in greenhouses peaches and nectarines are not so susceptible to it.

In last year's damp season many of my strawberries rotted away. How can I prevent this happening again?

Your strawberries were attacked by Botrytis, or Grey Mould as it is often called. It attacks a wide range of soft-tissued plants, appearing on fruits as well as on leaves and flowers. It is characterized by the appearance of a grey, fluffy mould that grows on the tissues. The fungus often enters the plant through cuts and damaged parts, and spreads rapidly in damp weather. Grey mould can quickly reduce strawberries to a rotting mass.

It can be controlled by removing affected parts as soon as they are noticed, and dusting or spraying the plants with benomyl or thiram.

OTHER PESTS AND DISEASES OF FRUITS

WOOLLY APHID
This well-known pest of apple trees is often called American Blight. It develops cottonwool-like fluffy tufts in cracks and crevices on the bark of apple trees, as well as on ornamental shrubs and trees such as pyrus, pyracantha, hawthorn and cotoneaster. Apply winter sprays of tar oil and summer sprays of dimethoate or malathion. Infected wood should be cut out and burned during winter pruning.

RASPBERRY CANE SPOT
It is frequently called Anthracnose and is a common complaint of raspberries, but not so serious as Cane Blight. It attacks raspberry, blackberry and loganberry stems or canes and seriously weakens the plants. Infection occurs in spring and the first sign of attack is noticed in early June when small purple or blue spots appear on the stems. These slowly elongate. Cut out and burn all infected canes after fruiting. Spray canes with benomyl or copper sprays.

AMERICAN GOOSEBERRY MILDEW
Stems, berries and leaves become covered with a fungus growth, white at first then dark brown. Shoots become stunted. In August cut out and burn all affected shoots. Spray with benomyl.

Q

Last year the cores of my apples became eaten away and rotten. There were small whitish grubs roaming around some of the fruits. And some of the fruits started to rot. What was the trouble with them?

A

Your apples were attacked by Codling Moth, a pest that also attacks pears, quinces and plums, causing maggotty fruits in July and August. Codling Moth, by the way, is often confused with Apple Saw Fly which occurs earlier. The caterpillars of Codling Moth usually enter the fruits at the top and produce a sawdust-like substance. Often, the holes made by this pest allow diseases to enter and attack the apples.

The Codling Moth lays its eggs on apple leaves and fruitlets from June to August. The eggs hatch and the young grubs eat the fruits. They leave the fruits in mid-August to pupate. This is a pest that can be controlled by using a general insecticide in late June and again in early July. The insecticide permethrin is very effective.

If you do not like spraying chemicals in your garden, you could try an old method of controlling Codling Moth: tie bands of sacking or corrugated cardboard around the trunk just below the branches. The caterpillars hibernate in cocoons in these bands during autumn, and in winter they can be removed and burnt.

PEAR LEAF BLISTER MITE

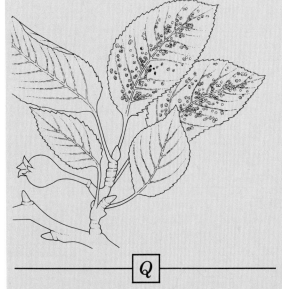

Left *Damage caused by Pear Leaf Blister Mite.*

Q

Last year the leaves on my pear tree were covered with yellowish markings which turned to black blisters. What was the problem?

A

These are the signs of Pear Leaf Blister Mite. Attacked leaves fall prematurely, and the young fruitlets become blistered. Spray the tree with lime sulphur in late March or early April, just as the buds open.

APPLE SCAB

Q

Every year my apples are covered with distorted, deformed, circular, blackish-brown areas. The leaves of the tree are also covered by a series of dark brown spots. What is the trouble?

A

Most certainly it is Apple Scab, a wide-spread fungal disease of apples. A related disease also attacks pears. It is worse during wet seasons, and trees can be infected any time during the growing period.

Fortunately, this disease can be controlled. Each autumn rake up all leaves and burn them. Several sprayings will be needed: benomyl,

thiram or bupirimate/triforine should be used when the green flower buds first appear, then at the pink bud stage, at petal fall, and again three weeks later.

TREES AND HEDGES

HEDGES

I live in a coastal area and want to plant a fast-growing coniferous hedge. What do you suggest?

The well-known Leyland Cypress x *Cupressocyparis leylandii* is widely planted in seaside gardens. It is the fastest growing hedge, but reaches a considerable size, up to 15 m (50 ft) in twenty or so years and eventually much higher. Set the plants about 750 mm (2½ ft) apart. If it is intended to form a shelter belt, set the plants in a staggered row, with the plants 1 m (3½ ft) apart. The golden form 'Castlewellan' displays brightly-coloured foliage and is ideal where a shorter hedge is needed. Set these plants 600 mm (2 ft) apart. Plant in September–November and keep watered if the weather is dry.

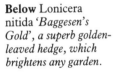

Below Lonicera nitida *'Baggesen's Gold', a superb golden-leaved hedge, which brightens any garden.*

Is it better to have a hedge with slightly inward sloping sides, than vertical?

Yes, as this shape helps to prevent the base becoming straggly and allows more light and air to reach the base. Another advantage of trimming hedges this way is that they are less likely to become damaged by heavy snow falls.

I have recently moved to an old house with a natural stone path down the centre of the garden. I want to plant a low, flowering hedge along either side of it. Is there a particular plant which will suit this purpose?

A plant which will harmonize with an old path in a cottage-garden setting is *Lavandula nana atropurpurea* (syn. *L.* 'Hidcote'). This is a compact and low-growing lavender, which achieves a height and width of 450–600 mm (1½–2 ft). It displays deep purple-blue flowers from July to September. The plants should be set 300 mm (1 ft) apart.

I want to plant a small, golden-leaved hedge with an informal outline. What do you suggest?

Lonicera nitida 'Baggesen's Gold' is a superb form, with golden leaves. It is best when left unclipped with a somewhat unkempt outline. It does best in full sun, where the good light brings alive the foliage. It grows to about 1·5–1·8 m (5–6 ft) high and 750–900 mm (2½–3 ft) wide. The plants should be set 300 mm (1 ft) apart.

Q

My wife yearns for a sweetly-scented old-fashioned rose hedge. Can you help?

A

The long flowering period and the sweetly-scented, semi-double, rich creamy-pink flowers of the Hybrid Musk 'Penelope' make it ideal as a hedge. Set the plants 750–900 mm (2½–3 ft) apart. This rose will form a hedge 1·5–1·8 m (5–6 ft) high and 1·2–1·5 m (4–5 ft) wide.

Another Hybrid Musk Rose to consider is 'Cornelia', which, with its coppery-apricot, scented blooms, also makes a lovely hedge. If the site is sunny these hedges will flower well and bloom throughout the summer.

Q

In my previous garden all of the hedges I planted eventually developed bare areas at their bases. I want to avoid this happening in my new garden. What should I do?

A

These bare bases occur because the plants were not properly pruned during their early months after being planted. During the first year it is essential to encourage plants to produce plenty of shoots from around their bases by pruning them as soon as they are planted.

Deciduous (leaf-shedding) kinds, such as beech, hornbeam and hawthorn, are cut back by a third to a half. This not only encourages bushiness, but reduces the amount of growth buffeted by winds that would otherwise loosen the plants in the soil. It also reduces the possibility of damage from heavy falls of snow during the first winter after planting.

Slow-growing evergreens which include Box (*Buxus sempervirens*) can be lightly tipped back after planting, but conifers should not be touched. However, formal evergreen hedging plants such as Privet and *Lonicera nitida* will need cutting back by one-third or half if the bases are to be kept full of growth and not to become bare during later years.

In old and neglected gardens hedges are often the first plants to get out of hand. There are then two solutions – first to cut the hedge hard back to see if it will create fresh shoots from ground level; and if not to dig it up, revitalize the soil and plant a fresh one.

Above *Hybrid musk rose 'Penelope' makes an attractive, informal hedge that is colourful throughout the summer.*

FLOWERING HEDGES

Berberis × *stenophylla*

An oustanding evergreen shrub with arching sprays of yellow flowers during May and June. Set the plants 600 mm (2 ft) apart. Clip the hedge after flowering, when it can be contained to 1·5–2·1 m (5–7 ft) high and 1–1·2 m (3½–4 ft wide. Suitable only for large gardens.

Escallonia '**Slieve Donard**'

A beautiful evergreen shrub with an arching habit and large arrangements of apple-blossom-pink flowers in June on the previous season's wood. Set the plants 750 mm (2½ ft) apart. As a hedge it can be restricted to 1·5–1·8 m (5–6 ft) high and 900 mm–1 m (3–3½ ft) wide.

Pyracantha rogersiana

An evergreen, erect, dense shrub with white flowers and masses of red berries. Set the plants 500 mm (20 inches) apart. When grown as a hedge it can be contained to a height of 1·2–1·8 m (4–6 ft) and a width of 900 mm (3 ft).

Rosmarinus officinalis '**Jessop's Upright**'

A delightful, erect, evergreen shrub with light mauve flowers mainly during spring. Set the plants 600 mm (2 ft) apart. It forms a hedge 1·2–1·8 m (4–6 ft) high and 900 mm (3 ft) wide.

Rhododendron luteum

A sprawling, deciduous shrub, ideal for an informal hedge in a wild garden. Its honey-suckle-like, scented, yellow flowers appear in June. Set the plants 750 mm (2½ ft) apart. It grows to 1·8–2·4 m (6–8 ft) high and 1·5–1·8 m (5–6 ft) wide.

TREES

Above *The spectacular*
Magnolia x
soulangiana.

 Q

Please recommend a small magnolia.

A

One of the most spectacular forms is *Magnolia ×
soulangiana*. It displays white, chalice-shaped
flowers 130–150 mm (5–6 inches) across, stained
light purple at their bases during April. After
twenty years it reaches 3·5–4·5 m (12–15 ft) tall
and 3·5–5·4 m (12–18 ft) wide. The form
'Lennei' has rose-purple flowers.

Magnolia stellata is another small magnolia,
rising to 2·4–3 m (8–10 ft) high and with a
spread of 2·4–3·5 m (8–12 ft). It is frequently
known as the Star Magnolia, producing white,
star-like 75–100 mm (3–4 inch) wide flowers during March and April. The form 'Rosea' displays
pink-flushed flowers, deep pink when in bud.

Q

At the bottom of my garden I want to plant a
tree that develops rich autumn colours in its
foliage. Have you any suggestions?

A

Perhaps the best known tree for vivid fiery tints
is the Sweet Gum (*Liquidambar styraciflua*). It
eventually develops into a large tree, but only
reaches 5·4–6 m (18–20 ft) after twenty or so
years. Its deeply-lobed leaves become brilliant
scarlet and orange in October and November
before falling.

Other superb autumn-colour trees include
carmine, orange and reddish-hued *Parrotia
persica* and *Cercidiphyllum japonicum* and flame-
tinted *Nyssa sylvatica*.

Shrubs with autumn colouring include reddish orange-leaved *Fothergilla monticola*, golden-
yellow tinted *Hamamelis mollis* 'Pallida', glow-
ing, red-hued *Rhus typhina* and many of the
small acers.

Q

Please suggest some trees with attractive
leaves in purple, cream or yellow.

 A

Some of the finest purples can be found amongst
the following trees: purple beech *Fagus sylvatica*
'Purpurea', a magnificent and large tree; Pis-
sard's Purple Plum (*Prunus cerasifera* 'Atropurpurea') which is more suitable for a small
garden; *Acer platanoides* 'Goldsworth Purple,'
and *Acer platanoides* 'Crimson King', resplendent with deep purple-crimson foliage.

Choice golden-leaved trees are *Robinia
pseudoacacia* 'Frisia', a delight with ferny leaves
on elegant branches, and *Gleditsia triacanthos*
'Sunburst', which is similar in appearance but
with more glossy golden leaflets. Again, its
shoots have a light, arching habit and it is
possible to underplant with shade-loving border
perennials.

Acer negundo 'Variegatum' has claim to fame
with its creamy-white margined leaves and white
bloomed new shoots. But it can revert, so green-
leaved stems must be removed the moment they
appear.

Can you recommend a tree for a very small front garden?

The Japanese Cherry *Prunus* 'Amanogawa' is ideal for a restricted area. It presents a narrow, columnar shape covered in April and May with semi-double, slightly fragrant, soft pink flowers. After twenty or so years, it reaches 5·4–6 m (18–20 ft) high with a spread of 1·5–1·8 m (5–6 ft). In its early years it is quite slim.

For a flowering cherry with a shrub-like habit, the Dwarf Russian Almond (*Prunus tenella* 'Fire Hill') is worth considering. It forms an attractive mound 900 mm–1.2 m high and wide. During mid-spring it reveals 12–18mm (½–¾ inch) wide bright rose-crimson flowers along the stiff stems. It is an ideal shrub for a narrow border, but make sure you position it in good light and where the soil is well drained.

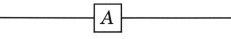

What is the Golden Rain Tree?

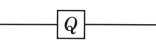

There are, in fact, two trees known by this common name. One is *Koelreuteria paniculata* from Asia, which displays yellow flowers in loose, large, terminal clusters during July. The other tree is the well-known Laburnum with its pendulous clusters of yellow flowers which bloom during May and June.

My local park has an Indian Bean Tree. I am told that there is a golden-leaved and smaller form, suitable for small gardens. Is this so?

The golden-leaved Indian Bean Tree is *Catalpa bignonioides* 'Aurea' and is, indeed, ideal for small gardens. It is deciduous and slow-growing, with large, heart-shaped, yellow leaves. During July it displays white flowers with yellow and purple markings. Try to position it so that the foliage is colour contrasted against darker leaved plants or even blue sky.

FLOWERING TREES FOR SMALL GARDENS

Shad Bush (*Amelanchier lamarckii*)
  Height: 3–4·5 m (10–15 ft)
  Spread: 3–3·5 m (10–12 ft)
A stunningly attractive deciduous tree with a profusion of star-shaped, white flowers in spring. Rich-coloured leaves in autumn.

Golden Rain Tree (*Laburnum × vossii*)
  Height: 4·5–6 m (15–20 ft)
  Spread: 3–3·5 m (10–12 ft)
A well-known tree, sometimes planted as a street tree, with spectacular pendulous bunches of pea-shaped, yellow flowers during May and June.

Flowering Crab (*Malus × lemoinei*)
  Height: 4·5–6 m (15–20 ft)
  Spread: 3·5–4·5 m (12–18 ft)
A beautiful hybrid crab with masses of single purple-crimson flowers in April and May. Other superb varieties include *Malus* 'Profusion' with single, deep-red flowers opening to purple-red – and *Malus* 'Snowcloud', an American double-flowered form with pure white blossom.

Below *The Indian Bean Tree* (Catalpa bignonioides *'Aurea'), a beautiful tree of great 'architectural' merit.*

LAWNS

LAWN TYPES AND CARE

---Q---

Please suggest types of hard-wearing grasses that I should ask to be included in a seed mixture for my lawn.

---A---

The types you need to ask for are dwarf strains of Perennial Ryegrass (*Lolium perenne*), Chewing's Fescue (*Festuca rubra commutata*) and the Crested Dog's Tail (*Cynosurus cristatus*). Usually, mixtures of seed for hard-wearing lawns are sold ready-mixed, and this is the easiest way of buying them, especially for a small area.

Mixtures of fine grasses based on Chewing's Fescue (*Festuca rubra commutata*) and Highland Bent (*Agrostis setacea*) for more decorative lawns are also sold, as well as mixtures containing Wood Meadowgrass (*Poa nemoralis*) for sowing in shady areas.

---Q---

I have bought a new house and plan to lay a lawn in my back garden. Is it better to make a lawn from seed or turf?

---A---

If you want an 'instant' lawn, then turf must be the answer. It is, however, about four times as expensive as seed, and the ground still needs thorough preparation to remove perennial weeds and to break up the top foot or so, to ensure drainage is good and the roots can easily penetrate the soil.

Eventually, lawns from seed are superior to those made from turf, and the type of grasses used can be selected to suit the lawn's uses. Hard wearing mixtures containing dwarf rye grass are the best choice if children are frequently using the lawn as a combat area!

LAWN REPAIRS

---Q---

When is the best time to apply weedkillers to lawns, and how should I do this?

---A---

Use weedkillers on lawns only when the grass is growing strongly. This is usually during late spring and summer. Do not apply it to grass that has suffered owing to dry weather. Make sure you do not use weedkiller on a windy day as there is a danger that it will drift on to healthy flowers and plants.

Stretch strings down the length of the lawn, 1 m (3½ ft) apart, and use a dribble bar (a perforated tube) on a watering-can to ensure accurate application.

Ideally, wear gloves for protection while using weedkiller and always wash your hands thoroughly afterwards.

Thoroughly wash the equipment after use, keeping it solely for the application of chemicals.

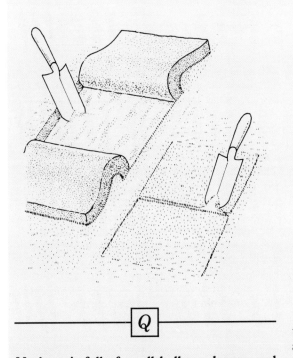

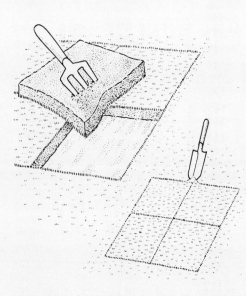

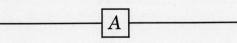

My lawn is full of small hollows, bumps and bare areas. Is it possible to rectify each little problem area to avoid digging up the entire lawn?

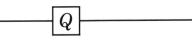

Yes, it is possible to level bumps and indentations. Use a sharp edging-iron to cut back strips of turf 230–300 mm (9–12 inches) wide. Peel back these strips – using a turfing-iron or spade – and either scrape out soil or fill in hollows.

Bare areas can be levelled and seed sown over the raked and prepared soil. If the weather is dry after sowing seed, water the soil and then place a sheet of clear polythene over it. Black polythene can be used, but has to be removed as soon as the seeds germinate.

Damaged patches can be re-seeded, or lifted and replaced with new turves. When laying new turves, firm well with a turf beater or the back of a spade. Water thoroughly and keep the area damp for two weeks to help the edges knit together neatly. If the edges of your lawn are damaged, use a sharp flat spade or edging-iron to cut out a piece of turf, then reverse it so that the damaged areas is towards the centre of the lawn. Fill the broken area with soil and re-seed.

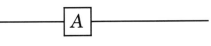

Is there any special system to follow when laying turf?

Yes. After thoroughly and evenly digging the soil and removing all perennial weeds, tread the soil to firm it and rake it to produce a level surface. When laying the turf, start by laying a row lengthways down one side. Turves can then be laid butting on to this, with the ends staggered so that they are not all in one line. This necessitates cutting some turves in half so the finished result compares with bonded bricks in a wall. Always use a half-moon edger to cut turves, as a spade will leave a scalloped edge.

LAWN MAINTENANCE

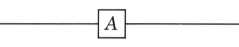

When should a lawn roller be used?

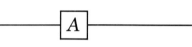

Once a year, to firm frost-lifted turf before the first spring cut. Then put it away. Over-use of a roller quickly compacts the soil, spoiling drainage and restricting aeration which leads to poor root growth.

Q

What is the best way to apply fertilizers to a lawn? I only have a small lawn and no special lawn equipment.

A

Above *To apply fertilizers evenly, stretch string at metre intervals, then space strips of wood at the same distance as you proceed.*

For large lawns a fertilizer distributor is the easiest way. But for small gardens the easiest method is to stretch strings 1 m (3½ ft) apart down the length of the lawn and then use two canes or strips of wood to form 1 m squares. Spread the fertilizer on a calm, damp day at the recommended rate for each square metre, then move one of the canes to form a further square.

Should I use a grass box on my mower, or let the grass cuttings remain on the surface?

There are reasoned arguments for both. Allowing the cuttings to remain on the lawn means that mineral nutrients are returned to the soil. Also, the cuttings help to conserve moisture in the soil during periods of drought. However, leaving the cuttings encourages earthworms to make casts on the surface, which may be unpleasant. Also, they tend to encourage diseases to attack the grasses. For a really picturesque lawn it is better to remove the cuttings.

Q

My cylinder-type grass mower produces an uneven cut – in bands across the lawn. What is the explanation?

A

It could be because of either the lawn or the mower. Check that the cylinder is in contact with the fixed bottom blade evenly across the width of the machine. Also, ensure that the cylinder and bottom blade are at a uniform height above the lawn's surface. Or it may be that the lawn is on a slope, and the weight of the machine is not evenly balanced, producing a closer cut on one side than the other.

How can I eliminate lawn moss?

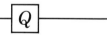

There are many proprietary moss killers currently available, usually based on dichlorophen or chloroxuron. Moss usually only occurs on wet, ill-drained lawns, so the best way to prevent the growth of moss is to improve drainage. Once a lawn is established it is difficult to improve drainage; this is why thorough drainage and soil preparation is essential when preparing the site for use as a lawn.

Q

Below *A sloping lawn can look very attractive and need not be difficult to maintain.*

What kind of material should I use to top-dress my lawn, and when should it be applied?

A

Top-dressing is best done in autumn. First, however, use a garden fork to aerate the soil by pushing it in deep all over the lawn. Alternatively, use a special hollow-tined lawn aerator, which takes out cores of soil. Brush these off the lawn and then use a birch broom or the back of a rake to spread and sweep into the lawn a mixture of clean sharp sand and peat in the ratio of ⅔ peat, ⅓ sharp sand.

Q

How do I cope with sloping land that I wish to form into a lawn?

A

As long as your land can be sloped evenly, differences in height over the entire area do not matter. Of course, it must be visually attractive and have adequate drainage, but there should be no problem in cutting the grass if you use a hover-type mower. Hand-pushed mowers and those with traditional motors tend to slip off steeply-sloped banks, whereas a hover-type can be trailed over the slope.

INDEX

Annuals, hardy and half-hardy 4, 6–7

Baskets, hanging 22, 23
Biennials 4, 6
Borders
  against wall 5
  mixed 4
  narrow 5
  planning 4
  self-supporting plants 5
  small, choice for 4
  staking 5
Bulbs, corms and tubers
  barrel planting 8
  foliage, dead 9
  for cutting 26
  ground carpet 9
  light soil 17
  rock garden 8
  summer and autumn flowering 18
  under trees 8, 20

Centipedes, beneficial 48
Children's gardens 28–9
Climbing and trailing plants 14–15
Coastal areas 21, 56
Colour all year 18–19
Conifers, sites and planting 21, 56

Drainage 31

Evergreens 11, 15, 17, 20, 21, 24, 30, 31
  hedges 57

Flower arrangers' choices 26–7
Foliage, decorative 5, 8, 11, 14, 15, 16, 20, 27, 29, 56, 58, 59
Frames and cloches 46
  cloches, special uses 6, 46
  early cropping 47
  glass v. plastic 47
  polythene tunnels 47
  suitable plants 46
  tomato ripening 46
Fruit 50–55
  pests and diseases 54–5
  soft 52–3
    black and red currants 52
    gooseberries 53–4
    loganberries 53
    raspberries 52, 53, 54
    strawberries 46, 52, 54
    training and pruning 53
  trees 18, 19, 30, 50–51
    bark ringing 50
    root pruning 50
    training 51
    types
      almond 54
      apple 30, 50–51
      cherry 18, 19, 51
      malus (crab) 19
      nectarines 51, 54
      peach 51, 54
      pear 30, 51, 55
      plum 50
      sorbus (rowan) 19

Grasses
  ornamental and herbaceous 26–7
Greenhouses
  hanging baskets in 23
  heating 44, 45
  shapes and types 44
  staging, need for 45
Ground carpet 17, 20, 22, 24–5
  bulbs and corms 8, 9

Hedges 56–7
  bare base areas 57
  conifers 56
  flowering 57
  laurel 31
  noise absorption 21
  roses 12, 57
  sloping inward sides 56
Herbaceous plants 4
  dividing and increasing 5
  flowers for cutting and drying 26, 27
  self-supporting and staking 5
Herbs
  bay, tub planting 42
  border, planting 43
  protection in frames and cloches 43
  seed growing
    Basil 42
    Borage 42
    Chervil 43
    Parsley 42, 43
    Sweet Marjoram 42
  types, bedding (all 43)
    Angelica
    Applemint
    Chervil
    Chives
    Mint (better in pots)
    Rosemary
    Spearmint
    Tarragon
    Thyme (lemon and common)
Houseplants 29

Insectivorous plants 28

Lawns and grasses 60–63
  hard-wearing 60
  laying, levelling and maintenance 29, 60–63
Limestone, Westmorland, laying 25

Perennials 4–5
Pests and diseases
  flowers 32–5
  fruit 54–5
  types
    Apple Scab 55
    Black Army, Bean Aphid, Blight,
      Dolphin and Fly 41, 48
    Blackspot 32
    Botrytis 32, 33, 54
    Cane Blight 54
    Capsid Bug 35
    Carrot Fly Maggot 49
    Caterpillars 49
    Celery Fly 41
    Chrysanthemum Eelworm 34
    Cockchafers 49
    Codling Moth 55
    Cutworm 48
    Cuckoo Spit 34
    Earwigs 34
    Greenfly 35
    Leaf-rolling Sawfly 33
    Leatherjackets 49
    Mildew 32, 53, 54
    Millipedes 48
    Onion Fly Maggot 49
    Peach Leaf Curl 54
    Pear Leaf Blister Mite 55
    Stem Eelworm 5
    Toadstools 33
    Turnip Flea Beetles 49
    Vine Weevils 34
    Whiteflies 49
    Woolly Aphid (American Blight) 54

vegetables 48–9
weedkillers 31
Poisonous plants 28
Ponds, plants round 18, 25
Prickly plants 21
Problems
  aspects 14, 15
  birds 39
  borders 4–5
  bulb foliage 9
  fences 7
  lush growth 36
  noise 21
  screening
    against wind 21, 30
    eyesores 15
  sea air 21
  staking 5
  traffic 21
  under trees 8, 20
  walls 14–15
  see also Pests and diseases

Restoring gardens 30–31
Rock gardens and dry walls 24–5
  elements for success 24
  stone sinks 22
Roof gardens 23
Root cuttings 5
Roses
  climbers and ramblers 13, 15
  cohabiting plants 13
  floribunda 13
  hedges 12, 57
  pests and diseases 32
  pruning 13
  scented 13, 15
  standards 13

Salt-resistant plants 21
Sandstone-laying 25
Scented plants, shrubs and trees
  6, 7, 10, 13, 14, 15, 59
Seed-raising 6–7, 28–9, 42–3
  drills 37
Shady areas
  annuals 7
  bulbs 8
  shrubs 20
  woodland carpet 9
Shrubs
  berried 11
  flowers, coloured 10, 16, 17, 24, 27
  foliage, decorative 11, 16, 20, 27
  late-flowering 10
  moving 30
  pruning 10, 31
  rock garden 24, 25
  scented 10, 14
  shady areas 20
  soil, acid 17
  soil, dry 16
Small gardens, flowering trees for 59
Soil types
  acid 17, 49
  clay 16
  cold and wet 14
  dry 16
  heavy 16, 32
  hydrangea, effect on 9
  identifying and testing 16, 36
  sandy 17, 20
  shrubs for 16–17
  treatment and mulching 16, 37
  wet 31, 32, 49

Toadstools 33

Trees, ornamental 18–19, 58–9
  for poor soil 20
  magnolia 58
  spring-flowering 18, 19
  weeping 19
  see also Fruit
Trelliswork cover 14–15
Tubs and barrels 8, 9, 42

Vegetable garden 36–41
  crop rotation 36
  crowbars, dibbers and trowels
    for planting 41
  dressings and feeds 36
  frames and cloches 46–7
  growing bags 37
  lifting and harvesting 40
  pests and diseases 41, 48–9
  planning 36
  seed drills 37
  types
    asparagus 38
    beans 37, 38, 41, 47, 48
    brassicas 36, 41, 48
    celery 41
    cucumbers 37
    lettuce 37, 38, 48
    marrows 39
    onions and leeks 37, 39
    parsnips and swedes 37, 39, 41
    potatoes 40
    radishes 40
    sweetcorn 41
    tomatoes 37, 39, 46

Wall covering 14, 15
Water plants, upright 25
Weeping trees 19
Wind, screening 21, 30
Window boxes 8, 22

ACKNOWLEDGMENTS

The following photographs were taken specially for Octopus Books:
Michael Boys 16; Jerry Harpur 21, 24, 27, 63; Octopus library 37 above; George Wright 12, 58.

The publishers thank the following for providing the photographs in this book:
A-Z Botanical Collection 10 below, 29, 40; Bernard Alfieri 7 above, 26; Pat Brindley 7 below, 17, 28, 40 left, 47 right, 51; R Corbin 30, 61; Edenlite Ltd 44; R. and C. Foord 48 right; Marion Furner 39 above, 49, 53, above; Derek Gould 20; Iris Hardwick Library 18; John Harris 45; David Hoy Publications 23 above, 31 above, 60, 62; George Hyde 34; Leslie Johns 42; Margaret McLean 3; Tania Midgely 6; Harry Smith Collection 4, 9, 10 above, 15, 19, 22, 24 above, 33 above, 35 above, 47 left, 48 left, 54, 55, 57, 59; Spectrum Colour Library 8; Michael Warren/Photos Horticultural 11, 14, 25, 50, 52, 56.

Illustrations: Allard Studios 5; Bob Bampton (The Garden Studio) 51; Paul Buckle and Terri Lawlor 13, 31, 43, 61; Roger Gorringe (R.P. Gossop) 38; Nicolas Hall 55; Hayward Art Group 45; Ed Roberts 48; Nina Roberts 46; Craig Warwick (Linden Artists) 37, 39, 41; David Wright 32, 33.